WALKING IN THEIR FOOTSTEPS

Nicola Jones

First published 2016
by Rowanvale Books Ltd
Imperial House
Trade Street Lane
Cardiff
CF10 5DT
www.rowanvalebooks.com

A CIP catalogue record for this book is available from the British Library.

ISBN: 978-1-910832-40-0

To Dad

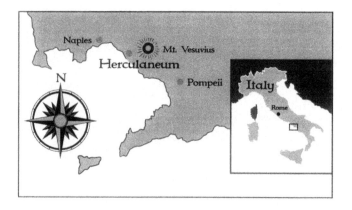

AUTHOR'S NOTE

Genealogy is an increasingly popular trend; my personal quest began when I was eleven years old. I would often listen with excitement to the stories my grandparents told of their childhood memories, reminiscing about their parents and moving events of family life during wartime. Events they spoke of were so clear and detailed to them, it is as if they had happened only yesterday. It left me wanting to know more about my ancestors behind the names, only saddened by not knowing their faces. Therefore, my quest began to bring these ancestors out of their black and white existence and bring them to life.

I never thought for a minute the hold it would grasp; a passion and thirst for knowledge of the past facilitated by my intrigue of the characters and times they lived in. I realised from an early age there is history all around us, determining our future.

What began like the dying embers of a fire; almost extinguished and forgotten, awaited more fuel to ignite and burn again. Reliving and sharing past memories with my grandparents produced times both pleasant and terrifying. Taking hold, they added fuel with their reminiscing and the flames flickered away almost into a blaze.

Then this life-changing event happened for both me and my dad. Hearing my dad's anxious story that day, I was left like many others, speechless, in awe of every detail he described. My fire continued to burn brighter than ever. Now my fire is an inferno, one that is way beyond my control, unable to be extinguished. One thing you learn very quickly about family history, there is no beginning or end, no boundaries and no limits to the branches you could explore. It just gets bigger and bigger, more challenging and intriguing.

Therefore, I have my dad to thank for this incredible journey of discovery. In addition, thanks go to those who shared our story at the beginning, giving us inspiration and encouragement to write this book for others to share.

We both thank you.

INTRODUCTION

Seeking warmth and comfort from our ignited fire, a treasure hunt begins. Old photographs emerging from once forgotten boxes, neglected over time. Faces not looked upon for many years... So precious are these mementos. They enable us to connect faces to names, though sadly some remain a mystery, family resemblances with no identity. Still wanting more than faces, you are inspired to discover their occupation, places they once inhabited, their loved ones and the era in which they lived. You contemplate their difficult times and the hardships they must have endured.

One day, I realised the information I had unearthed about people long-gone required some order. There was a need to share my treasure, to give warmth and comfort to others. I set about recording even the smallest of detail for future generations to recall and one day continue to find out about. Lessons learned along the way are truly inspiring, and they gave me an overwhelming appreciation of how lucky we are today, along with a great sense of where I came from and where I belong. Although we take many material goods for granted, and our economic crisis looks grim at present, our ancestors endured in eras that were much more severe.

Today, we can easily forget how rich we really are, with a roof over our heads, warm clothing, food in our bellies, our family and loved ones around us with their health of utmost importance... We are very rich indeed. Along with our environment, we take for granted our education, transport, the material goods in our home, the many labour-saving devices giving us much more free time — all great luxuries. If our ancestors could see such riches, they'd believe we were all millionaires.

Having experienced first-hand the departed spirit of deceased loved ones, I'm a firm believer that there's life after death — The presence of earth-bound spirits living amongst us. Anything supernatural, the unexplained, is frowned upon by sceptics. I myself was also sceptic until the day I was proven wrong by the other side. So, writing this book was a real adventure to get my teeth stuck into; combining the living, the past, the supernatural and deceased ancestors.

There are many strange and unexplainable things that can happen in one's lifetime. This story will certainly go down in our family history as one of them. It's a tale of true events, and it began by discovering a real find or two. An eventful year to follow with dreams and journeys spanning time, across land and sea. Each event is a link in the chain, connected to the next event. There will be some back and forth of time elements; it seems to make sense this way, rather than rearranging them into their chronological order and spoiling the twists and turns along the way.

Those who believe in the supernatural will be wowed by one man's journey; non-believers enthralled by the possibilities of the historical elements. This will open a plausible debate.

It is my belief, as I'm sure is true of others, that we all leave our footprints on the land, leaving our mark in different forms. Those before us were no different, and left their mark on the landscape — some more visible than others. Some facts have been proven through archaeological discoveries; others remain a mystery. Each of us have our own opinions on these mysteries, as there is very little evidence surrounding them and even historians can't agree on a single theory to explain them.

Much like those visible markings, I believe there are those most of us can't see — those of a spiritual nature. So, are these footprints crying out to be discovered? Or will we carry on asking ourselves: why?

The fact that this is my dad's story makes it all the more special. A life-changing experience that needed recording, another story to share. I agonised over how to write this book, not wanting to novelise or romanticise events. I resolved to represent exactly what happened and have the events speak for themselves. Some dialogue has been added, mostly because the events were only shown like a silent movie, although there was a sense of what could have been said. There was only true dialogue when both Dad and spirit were in physical connection. The names of the main characters were given by the spirits themselves. The names in italics were given after a little research and discussion with Dad to ensure they stayed true to the essence of the characters he met.

DREAMS

29th April to 4th May 2007.

Back in the spring of 2006, one of Dad's usual visits to the cemetery to tend family graves was distracted by the sound of singing and music. At first he thought he was hearing things; it wasn't choir singing or music coming from the nearby church — the sound was more distant. Barely audible, but very celestial, 'heavenly choirs of angels' was the only way he could describe it! Even though it was both pleasant and calming it sent shivers down his spine and distracted his thoughts. Was it an omen, a premonition maybe of things that were to come?

He heard the music on several separate occasions; each time he listened more carefully, but could never identify the words, as hard as he tried. The fact that he was the only person to hear it worried him. My mother was unable to hear anything. It stopped after August of that year and was never heard again.

It was the end of an exceptionally mild day in April. After making the most of the nice weather in the garden, busily preparing the ground for spring, planting his vegetable plot, Dad fell into much-needed sleep. He had a dream which began with an eerie mist; appearing from beyond the murky haze were two unfamiliar faces. There was an intense feeling that these souls were lost and forlorn... Their loneliness was disturbing. Dad awoke, and their poignant sadness left him agitated and restless. Glancing at the clock, he saw it was 4am. The house was silent and still. He was reluctant to return to sleep and return to the dream that played repeatedly in his mind; the images of the faces were still clear in his mind. Who were they?

The following night, he fell asleep once again; there was no thought of the previous night's dream. Experiencing the same mist, the faces were pretty much the same yet much clearer. However, they were still strangers. He was able to distinguish this time an adult and the small form of a female child, lost in the fog. Just standing there in front of him, they neither spoke nor moved. Having seen them the previous night, they felt more familiar to him; they did not appear to be so disturbing. He was awoken suddenly from the dream, by what, he didn't know. The time was exactly 4am.

For a third and fourth night, faced with the same recurring dream, it was as if Dad almost expected them to be there when he fell asleep. Each night they stayed a little longer in the dreams; they no longer felt like strangers but had an unusual familiarity about them. Beyond doubt, he was aware they had a connection to him. Why, he was not certain, but he sensed as much. The child reached out her hand, beckoning… He noticed on the back of her hand a familiar birthmark. Some recollection in his memory told him he'd seen this mark before. Strangely, her hand also had six fingers — another distinguishing feature.

Dad wondered at first if this is what it felt like to die in your sleep. Was she there to meet him, to take him to the other side? Having no wish to go with her, he withdrew his hand, waking himself up this time. It was still dark, the time again, 4am... Fearing the worst, this dream left him feeling terrified once again. Never before had he woken up at exactly the same time, four nights in a row. Mindful of the waking time he'd checked the clock, which was working perfectly. So was the time a significant factor or just a coincidence?

Baffled and tormented, trying to make sense of it all, Dad questioned himself, trying to recall where he'd seen the birthmark before. The dream had felt so real to him. His conclusion and only explanation: it was some kind of message, maybe from relatives who'd passed on. Having had his conscience pricked, he remembered his late father's dying wish.

'Look after my brother, watch out for him.'

Dad had promised to do so. Dad's uncle is one year older than him, and is my grandfather's only remaining sibling. A little more at ease, feeling he'd made sense of it all, he made time to visit his uncle.

He told him of the strange dreams he'd had over the past four nights. His uncle described the family birthmark as belonging to his recently departed sister Morita, inherited from her mother, Violet. This explained why Dad had recollections of its familiarity. His uncle, Tony, also has the same birthmark, which he showed him — only his was on his torso. During their conversation, his uncle mentioned that Morita's granddaughter had just lost a baby. 'There was meaning to the dream with the loss of a loved one and child; hence the presence of an adult spirit along with a female child spirit.' The idea that the dream was a visit from his aunt, so that she could receive the lost granddaughter into the kingdom of heaven, made the dreams easier to accept. Their familiarity made him feel safe. Mystery solved, conscience eased, job done. Surely, this would break the pattern of the dreams. He didn't expect any more visits; there was acknowledgement and closure.

What had been curious about these dreams had been the fact he had been able to remember them so clearly. By morning, most dreams are vaguely remembered, if at all, their clarity and details gone. So why did these dreams remain so clear, continuing to appear as a reminder at every quiet moment during the day?

Troubled for yet another night, he was revisited by the same dream, confused but feeling safe to stay longer. This time he stretched out to the beckoning child, sensing that all they wanted him to do was reach back!

As they joined hands, he was awoken once again — the time, 4am.

SUPERNATURAL

Saturday 5ᵗʰ May 2007.

The following morning, Dad woke with a sense of relief; the fear that was felt in the dream had not amounted to anything. It was the end of a strange and very restless week.

The weather had been particularly kind of late, but was somewhat changed on this day, becoming grey and overcast. Going about his usual Saturday routine — a little shopping and some family visits — Dad was bothered by a muzzy headache and felt relieved to get home after what seemed a very long day. It turned a little chilly towards evening and Dad's usual evening wander around the garden certainly called for a coat. As he tended his plants and generally pottered about, in need of some fresh air to clear his head, the dreams played clearly in his mind.

As he approached the lower end of the garden, he suddenly stopped, frozen to the spot. Unable to move, assuming his arthritis was playing up worse than usual, he was a little concerned.

Suddenly, an odd sensation washed over him. Turning around, he started walking — he had no control of his own legs and was unable to stop! He passed the kitchen window where he saw my mum inside, watching television. Scared, he called out to her, but found he was unable to speak! He continued up the front path, through the front gate. Where on earth was he going? He had no idea. He urged himself to stop, not understanding why he couldn't.

For a while, there seemed to be no one around — then, a familiar figure in the distance. Dad was relieved to see it was a neighbour of his. He tried to communicate, the words in his head unable to reach his mouth. The neighbour walked on by as if he were invisible. How strange, he thought, usually they would have stopped to pass the time of day, or say hello. He had an eerie feeling of being gently pushed along... but where was he going?

Soon it became clear where he was headed: the cemetery. He had often taken the short, familiar walk to tend the family graves. Once inside the churchyard, he was urged to take the familiar route, the main avenue of well-established trees either side. Suddenly it became very cold, so icy cold, his face felt brittle, sure to crack if it got any worse. The temperature made it a struggle to walk; pain flooded his lungs as he breathed in the freezing air. It became more and more difficult to walk as he continued, desperately hoping to get out of this perishing weather soon. He managed to walk through the bitter air, suddenly stumbling into brilliant sunshine. He had to shut his eyes momentarily, it was so dazzling. He revelled in the warm sensation of the sun on his face, joined by a warm breeze. These were physical sensations, not imagined.

Due to the inexplicable feeling, he no longer assumed his arthritis was to blame. Strange thoughts of the unknown entered his head. Being a sceptic, with no belief in the unknown, he was no longer sure what was controlling his movements.

Squinting, he allowed his eyes to adjust to the brightness. He started questioning whether he was still on Earth. Stood still now, with his eyes fully focussed, he was surprised to find that he was on a hill; it rose to his left and fell away to the right. The view ahead was unusual, yet he was standing in the familiar space of the cemetery. It was unusual because the familiar sight of the gravestones that should lie ahead had vanished. Instead, he was faced with an open landscape of the cemetery, as if in another era. It had a surreal painted quality, the colours blending together on a palette much brighter than usual, like those seen in a cartoon. The sun appeared huge in the background, seated on the horizon, three times larger than a normal setting sun. So close, it seemed almost reachable.

On the move again, he was being drawn up the hill. It was somehow possible to look directly at the sun without hurting his eyes. In the sun the silhouette of a huge figure of a man stood; from head to toe it was plain to see his immense size. Nevertheless, this was no dream; being fully awake, he was aware of the strange aura of this man and his surroundings.

Whilst it had been dusk when he left the house around six, the vision before him was as bright as midday, with brilliant white clouds. The silhouetted figure became clearer. Unexpectedly, a ball of blue light sped towards him, sent from the figure. Dad anticipated the blow and lowered his head, shrugging his body. He closed his eyes momentarily and it struck him between the stomach and chest. Hunched over the ball, and taken off his feet with the force, he hurtled backwards down the hill. From this action, he didn't fall to the ground as expected, but stopped in mid-air, inches above the ground. He was lowered gently until he felt solid ground beneath his feet.

Faced with the sun again, he felt some invisible force was at work. His constant thought was of how to get away, back to his family. The scenery behind was the same as that in front of him. With his feet now firmly planted on the ground, he was unable to move — there was no chance of escape.

Again, with no control over his actions, he was being pushed up the hill with what seemed like a similar force. He experienced pains in his chest, and his heart was pounding so loud he could feel it in his ears. Given the stress of the situation, it was quite possible he was experiencing an angina attack. He felt unwell as he searched for his relief spray. Struggling, his chest still in pain and distress, an aching in his legs, he was continually moved onwards.

Now feeling dizzy with pain, he was spun around by these opposing forces. Something certainly did not want him there — yet something else certainly did, and insisted on drawing him nearer. The dizziness eventually led to his physical collapse. Dad sat awhile, with his eyes shut, thinking to himself if he could not see them, they wouldn't hurt him.

Afraid of what he would see next, he realised there was no more pain.

Dad feared the worst; had he suffered not an angina attack, but a heart attack? At this point, he assumed he was on the other side. Feeling distressed, the thought of never seeing his family again drove more fear and pain into his heart. However, he could feel himself physically breathing and the solidness of the ground below. He had no idea where he was.

Opening his eyes, he was caught by the dazzling brightness again. Everything looked the same as before. Although in the cemetery, the usual gravestones that belonged in the present world were not present here, in what seemed to be the past. He assumed at this point that whatever was responsible had done what they wanted and he'd been put back to the place at the top of the hill.

One thing was different: the figure and strange aura of the tall man had vanished, nowhere to be seen. Being drawn up again, there was no sense of an opposing force. Standing upright, he felt afraid again; he was not alone, he felt another presence. Slowly but apprehensively, he turned to face two figures — the very same figures that had appeared to him in his dreams. Were they angels?

Comforted at least by their familiarity and sense of calm, the fear inside him had subsided. Their faces appeared much clearer than in his dreams, yet their bodies remained only as ghostly apparitions. Still looking around, he wondered where the other figure had vanished to and whether or not he was the dark side of death. His disappearance had certainly presented a sense of relief.

The child hid shyly behind the male figure; she also seemed wary of what was happening. Only her face was visible. A few moments passed before she was brave enough to come out of hiding. The figures appeared as if a silvery, blue energy pulsed through them. Dad felt overwhelmed with the events that led him here, but relieved that he'd been met by what he assumed were angels. Although relieved that he was with those on the right side and not with the evil presence that had lurked nearby, he was unable to forget about the dark figure. He wondered if he would reappear at any moment. As he looked over his shoulder in the direction of the sun, there was no sign of him.

After a few moments standing face to face, Dad asked them, 'Who are you? What do you want? You're the faces in my dreams. Are you angels?' His voice remained calm and steady, yet he felt anything but.

Their expressions showed they had heard his voice, but they looked puzzled, not understanding him.

'Am I dead?' Dad continued. 'Are you angels? What do you want with me?'

The child came out from hiding behind her companion but continued to hold his hand. She was only a child — a pretty child — and didn't appear frightening in the least. She held out her other hand to reach for Dad's. The first thing he noticed was the birthmark and her six fingers, just like in the dreams.

By now the pains in his chest had gone. At this time, he still didn't know whether he was alive or dead. Had his dreams been a premonition of this day? And were they here to greet him? With mixed feelings and apprehension, he reached out — he felt he had nothing to lose.

Deep down he hoped he was alive, and this was some sort of dream... His thoughts were of his family; the last thing he wanted was to leave them. He still felt dubious and anxious, but he no longer feared the 'angels'. His only worry was where they might take him next. He reached out to the child's beckoning hand, as he felt the need to move the situation forward. He remembered his dream; no harm had come to him then. He felt safe in their presence.

Hands now joined, he felt a warm, tingling sensation — much like static electricity — creeping up his arm and into his chest, through his legs, the communication floodgates opened. No verbal conversation took place; the following story was told through telepathy. The connection of hands, via the child acting as a mediator, made sure that the language spoken was understood by all.

'My name is Cateus,' replied the man, answering the questions. 'This is my daughter, Hygieia.'

'We are sorry for causing you worry,' Hygieia said. 'Please don't fear us — we mean you no harm. We can assure you you're not dead.

'You're safe with us!' insisted Cateus.

'Will you help us?'

CATEUS' STORY

Saturday 5th May 2007.
ERA 47AD – 79AD.

Dad was certain they were telling the truth. After such events, what were the other possibilities? If what they said was true, and he was not dead, then they couldn't be angels. Confused and traumatised, he now faced one question: how could he help them?

He wondered whether he had any choice in the matter.

'If I'm not dead, then where am I? What is this place?' he asks, posing the many questions running through his head. 'What are you?'

The male figure spoke once again; Dad hadn't imagined it before and he wasn't dreaming. For sure, we know the time of day was early evening; it was six o'clock when he left the house, so he was certainly not in his bed or even at home. 'What I'm going to tell you is my story. You will know in your heart who I am, and what I tell you is true,' Cateus replied. 'You are a good man, and I know you will help us...'

Cateus began to tell his story in his own words.

'I was born a slave in the year you will know as 47AD, in the Northern regions of Hispania. My mother Calla was a mere child herself at the age of fourteen when I was born; she was also a slave. As a child, she'd been sold into slavery, with no memories of her life before. I grew up not knowing my father; curious, I had once asked my mother about him. She told me I would know when the time was right.'

Cateus said he hadn't felt disadvantaged; there were many other children in the same situation. Although they were slaves, he told of a good life they shared. They had been well looked after and were happy.

'My master was no ordinary Roman, he was a very important man. His name was Servius Galba, Governor of Hispania. He was a general in the Roman Army commanding the fourteenth Legion. Galba was a man in his senior years, suffering from many ailments. One of my jobs was fetching the healers, much to my delight. Every moment of my spare time I would spend with them, learning and working with them, helping out where I could to gain knowledge. Their work fascinated me. They encouraged my interest, sometimes letting me help with more intricate surgery.'

Intrigued by their work, Cateus felt inspired by the healers. He hoped to become a surgeon himself; often he would share his thoughts with his mother. He wondered if he'd ever have the opportunity of becoming a healer, being a mere slave.

'Galba had also become aware of my fascination and ability in medicine,' Cateus continued. 'It was he who decided it would be a good idea to have his own healer to hand constantly. Therefore, I was sent to Greece to be educated in the field of medicine.

'I was nine when I was sent to Epidaurus in Greece to study and fulfil my dream of becoming a healer. For my journey and safekeeping, my mother gave me a gift — a coin. I carried it around my neck in a small pouch. If anything were to happen to me, it would have been my payment to the ferryman, ensuring safe passage across the river Stix and to Elysium... our Heaven. It was while I was at Epidaurus, having completed many years of training and grown into a young man, that I heard the news of my Master Galba and his newly appointed position as Emperor of Rome. It was good news — it was a far better position to be a slave of an emperor. I was happy for my mother and me; life would be even better. It meant a move to Rome for my mother.

'Unfortunately, our happiness was short lived and news reached me some months later of Galba's assassination. His reign as emperor was a short one. My thoughts were for my mother. I wanted to go to Rome immediately and find her. I had never been to Rome myself and had no idea what had become of her. Those around the Emperor would usually suffer the same fate: at best, she would be captured and sold back into slavery.

'My mentors would not allow me permission and persuaded me to stay and complete my education for my own safety. Deep down I knew they were right; my studies were almost complete, to throw it all away would have been foolish; my dreams would have been shattered, and to return would mean only slavery...but my mother, my dear mother!

'When my studies were completed and I qualified as a healer and surgeon, my thoughts were only for her. I had to travel to Rome and look for her there. I was finely dressed, the proud owner of a set of surgeon's instruments, when I took passage on a cargo ship. The journey was long and the ship had the misfortune of being attacked by pirates. The goods on board were of great value, and with the ship being so well laden we were slowed down, unable to outrun them. I was still a young man and not a soldier; therefore, I had no fighting experience and was scared for my life.

'"Your only chance of survival is to convince them you're the son of a wealthy man," were the words of the captain.

'"But... I'm not wealthy," I replied.

'"If you're caught you will be killed. It's your only chance — they will hold you captive, and it'll buy you some time," replied the captain.

'I feared the worst — death was surely upon me. I did as the captain told me — first I hid amongst the cargo. Pirates overran the ship. I listened to the agony and chaos of the battle from my hiding place. The cries of anguish from a bloody and brutal fight were all I heard. There had been much bloodshed. I felt helpless and thought I should help the wounded, but I remained hidden and frightened.

'I only appeared to be wealthy by the way I dressed. My only possessions in the world were my instruments and the coin I carried around my neck.

'It seemed a long time before there was the sound of order and calm. I had a fair idea the ship was under a new command. When found, they took my only possessions, my coin and instruments made of precious metal. The remainder was thrown across the floor with such disregard it filled me with heartache. I pleaded with my captors to take me to their captain.

'I feared I would die before I could see my mother again. Remembering my captain's words, I knew what I had to do and lied. I told the pirate leader of my family back in Rome, of the wealth and fortune they would pay for my safe return. The reward was enough for them to agree to keep me alive.

'They enquired as to my reason for being aboard the ship and my profession. It was realised that I might be of some use, and they set me to work treating their wounded. The injuries were numerous and severe. I only agreed to help on the condition my instruments were returned in order to begin treatment. I was kept very busy whilst on board the ship; most of the crew received treatment at some stage of the journey.

'I was eventually regarded as a friend, and the pirates treated me fondly as part of their crew. A year had passed since I had set out to find my mother, and I hoped she was still alive and safe. Some of my friends knew that I had to find my mother and had realised I wasn't the wealthy man they had assumed. They promised to say nothing to their captain, as I was still of use to them as a surgeon. I had one true friend whom I trusted. A young Jewish boy named *Jacob*.

'*Jacob*, aware of my growing unhappiness, helped plan my escape. We had to wait for a change in the weather. Somehow, he had managed to retrieve my stolen coin, unknown to me at this time.

'The weather had changed and the ship sailed off the coast of Italy. Filled with eagerness and anticipation we waited as night fell and the ship was silent, as we lowered a small boat into the water. *Jacob* placed the coin in my hand as a parting gift; I could not believe my eyes. To be reunited with my mother's gift was like having part of her back.

Words failed me; the dread of now being alone was ahead of me; thoughts of losing my one true friend, never to see him again, consumed me.

"'Come with me!' I pleaded. "It'll be a new life for both of us."

'Neither of us wanted the friendship to end, but both knew this was our final farewell.

'I pleaded once more, "Please, come with me?"

"'I can't leave with you, this is my life, the only one I know!" was his reply.

'We had a final embrace before I bid farewell, knowing in our hearts we would never see each other again. Both of us were grateful to have shared each other's friendship.

'After many hours spent drifting and rowing, I was relieved to reach land, on the coast of Italy. I began my journey to Rome immediately. When I reached the city, I thought the only way to remain undetected whilst I searched for my mother was to set up as a surgeon. I used the money I had received through my share as a pirate to set up a surgery, and knew it would be a means of earning a legitimate wage.

'I had waited a long time before the day I had dreamt of finally arrived. I was called to a house to treat a sick man, a slave. I recognised him immediately; he had lived in my village when I was a child. He didn't recognise me now, as I'd grown into a man. At first I was afraid of being identified — I feared telling him my identity. Surely, the risk of me still being a slave to the house of Galba would mean death. It was a difficult choice to make but I was eager to find my mother so telling him was a chance I had to take.

'It was fortunate that he had indeed remembered my mother and me. Thankful for his treatment, he agreed to keep my identity secret. More importantly, he knew of my mother's whereabouts. "She lives at Galba's villa in Herculaneum, sent there for her own safety."

'It was such a relief to hear she was still alive. I packed up my belongings and headed for Herculaneum. Once there, it was not difficult to find her and we were happy to be reunited at last. She told me, "When Galba became Emperor of Rome, he gave us our freedom."

'We were no longer slaves! She'd fled Rome because of her connection with Galba. Furthermore, she felt it was time to tell me of my father. My father was indeed my former master, Galba. This explained why my mother had been given the villa at Herculaneum. We were now citizens of Rome.

'Could this news possibly have been another reason that a young slave boy was sent to Epidaurus and given the opportunity to be educated, allowed to make something better for himself and his future?

'I had found happiness again; I was finally reunited with my mother. I set up another surgery at Herculaneum and could not have been happier.

'At the age of twenty-two, in 69 AD, there had been trouble rising. It was a time when Rome was invading Britain. It was my compulsory duty to join the Roman Army, as all citizens of Rome did. I wanted no part in the troubles, but my only option was to be a soldier or a coward. I was now able as a free citizen of Rome to join as an officer and a surgeon, and hence came to Britain with my legion. We eventually came here to Gelligaer, setting up an auxiliary fort. Being the only surgeon, I spent my spare time visiting the surrounding villages, helping the wounded and those who needed medical attention. The local villagers were not keen on me at first — after all, I was a Roman and therefore their enemy. It was not in my nature to harm anyone but it took some time before they began to trust me.

'The village population consisted of mostly the elders, women and children. The men were out in the hills, preparing for battle, in readiness to protect their people — those that hadn't been press ganged into the Roman Army. There was much sickness that plagued the village and I did all I could to help fight any further spread and contamination.

'With the fort being so close to the village, they were very much under the occupation of the Romans, and were no more than mere slaves. There was a great divide; the villagers kept their distance as best they could from their invaders, fearing their control and power. A young woman named *Medica,* who was tending the sick and her family, seemed to be at the top of the hierarchy of the village; and also was initially very wary of my help. As time passed and they observed my care and healing, their opinions of me changed. *Medica* herself was eager to help her people be provided with the much needed aftercare to aid recovery.

'Our friendship soon blossomed into a relationship that was kept secret from her kinfolk. We both knew our love was forbidden, being enemies. *Medica* could not help her feelings; she knew I was different through my dedication and care for her people. We married in a secret grove, in the tradition of her people, after eventually receiving her father's blessing. The binding of our hands in symbolic union joined us as one. I wrote and told my mother of the news and of how happy I was, promising to return home soon. I never lost my close bond with my mother; despite being so far away, she remained always in my heart. I would write to her as often as I could.'

Up until this point in the story, Dad had only been able to hear the spirit's spoken words. When Cateus spoke of the events in Gelligaer, Dad was able to sense feelings and emotions, and could actually see the said events in his mind's eye.

'*Medica* fell pregnant with our first child,' Cateus continued, 'and both of us could not have been any happier. The months passed by quickly, busy in our care for others. When the day arrived and *Medica* went into labour, I was on duty at the fort and unaware of the event. She would be in the capable hands of the experienced women. Concern amongst the women grew during delivery and there seemed no sign of the child being born despite their efforts. With *Medica* weakened by the labour and complications worsening, I was called for. Immediately I recognised both mother and baby were in danger; to save them both I had to work fast. The cord had wrapped around the baby's neck and I rectified this at once. The labour had been long and exhausting for both *Medica* and the child. She was very weak and feared I would lose her.

'My main attention was to tend to my wife whilst I passed

the baby to the women. *Medica* kept asking for the child; when I looked over to the women I knew something was wrong. The look on their faces said it all as they shook their heads. I rushed across and saw the limp body, not breathing. She appeared to be dead. Taking hold of my daughter in my arms, I cleared her airways whilst the women watched curiously. They were confused when I asked for a bowl of hot water and another of cold. I initiated by breathing into her mouth, inflating the tiny lungs, then plunged her into the cold water, followed by the hot water, and repeated this action once again, until she cried out — much to my delight. The women in attendance looked on as if I had performed some kind of evil magic. It led them to believe the child was special, having been brought back from the dead.

'Life was good being a father, and *Medica* made a full recovery. Our daughter was perfect in every way, but oddly possessed six fingers on each hand — something I had never seen before. The villagers and *Medica* saw this as a sign of great power. In my next letter to my mother I wrote of our great joy and arrival of our daughter, how when my service was complete I would bring my family home with me and how I looked forward to seeing her once again.

'A special child like our daughter deserved a special name: Hygieia. I named her after a goddess, the Greek goddess of healing, whom I'd once worshipped during my training as a young boy. Hygieia was a deity worshipped at Epidaurus; she was the daughter of Asclepius, god of healing.

'Whilst growing up and watching her I noticed Hygieia had a special gift, one that neither of us could understand. With each year that passed, her inbuilt knowledge and gift increased. It was an ability that was so natural to her young age; she had the power to heal and mend that was quite unlike the one I had taken many years to learn. A friend of hers had fallen from a tree, breaking the bone in her leg. Instinctively using her hands, she placed them on the leg and miraculously healed the broken bone.

'After witnessing the event, I decided to let her help me with my work, giving her the guidance she needed and keeping a close eye on her skill. *Medica* was also aware of Hygieia's gift and had known others like her before. Fascinated by her ability to be at one with nature, she had the same gift with animals and she had great knowledge of plants and their healing and medicinal properties.

'Hygieia would often go out with her basket to collect such plants, one day she'd been gone sometime so I went to look for her. When I came across her in the woods playing with some wolf cubs, I feared for her safety and was about to step out. I was sure their mother would return and harm Hygieia in order to protect her young, when to my amazement the mother and other adult wolves were already close by. She seemed to be in no danger as she played and I watched with joy, until she picked up her basket affectionately bidding the young cubs' farewell to return home.

'In her seventh year, Hygieia was out walking with her grandfather, *Cradog,* when she was distracted by a giant of a man. Only she seemed able to see him. She spoke of him to her grandfather, curious as to who he was.

'"What did he look like?" her grandfather asked.

'Hygieia described him and *Cradog* immediately recognised him as Bran. Bran had left the village for some twenty years ago. This was a bad omen, he felt, and took Hygieia's hand to return to the village immediately. That evening, *Cradog* sat alone outside his home. He sensed that Bran was close by but was unable to see him. He called out, "I know you're there — show yourself... Why are you hiding?"'

As Bran appeared into the vision, Dad recognised this figure as the silhouette seen earlier in the sun, the very being that had pushed him away. A sudden fear washed over him again, and he hoped that he could not be seen by him.

Dad shook himself as Cateus continued his story. '*Cradog* looked upon the face of Bran, not understanding what he saw. It had been twenty years since they last met, yet he hadn't aged at all; Bran still had his boyish looks, yet *Cradog* was an old man. Bran asked *Cradog* of his daughter *Arianwyn*. Still confused, *Cradog* replied, "She's dead."

'"When? How?" Bran replied, grief-stricken.

'"She died of a broken heart not long after you left; you

should have taken her with you." The memory was all too painful still for *Cradog*.

"'I couldn't take her where I was going, it was no place for her!" answered Bran.'

Cateus then explained to Dad that Bran was a Celt but also a Druid. 'He had returned to the village after twenty years. He was of a different race, hence his huge size — almost twice my size. He'd returned and was angered to find the Romans in control of his village — he hated Romans. What had angered him more was that his people were moving away from their own beliefs and gods and beginning to worship those of the Romans.

'Bran was infuriated and told his people they had angered the gods with their behaviour of becoming Romanized. The younger villagers seemed not to know who Bran was and took no notice of him, fearing the Romans more. However, the village elders knew all too well of Bran's powers and capabilities. They knew of the magic he possessed and deemed him invincible.

'Bran began to whip the villagers into a frenzy, giving them a warning to change their ways or else the sun god would leave the sky. There was no response from them, so he plunged them into darkness with the threat that the light would never return. It was then that *Cradog* stepped up to plead with his people, urging them to listen to Bran, warning them he had far more power than all the Romans and should be listened to.'

Dad witnessed the darkness; there was not a star in the sky. There was only the distant sound of thunder, the sky lit occasionally by lightening. He sensed that it had remained dark for many days.

'The villagers were very frightened of Bran's prediction coming true; there was rioting amongst them and much distress. All soldiers were put on duty to calm the situation.

'Bran's powers were realised; those that had ignored him were now eager to listen, asking him what they must now do to please the gods. Bran told them the thunder god was angered and could only be pleased by human sacrifice. He said that when the light returned they must raise an army to drive the Romans out and return the land to the old ways. Bran was then told of me helping the villagers and my family, especially that of Hygieia and how they call her "the special one". Bran convinced his people that, as a Roman, I had bad magic. He continued to tell them the prophecy could only be ended with a human sacrifice: the pure life of the one they call "the special child", with hair the golden colour of sun and eyes of sparkling blue...

'Having found Hygieia, despite feeling guilty about their actions, they gave her something to drink, some kind of potion that made her unconscious, before offering her to Bran. Bran took her to the "Stone of Kings" (known today as "Maen Catwg"), followed anxiously by *Cradog* pleading him not to harm her. He was knocked to the ground by Bran. When Bran reached the stone she was lain upon it and in the blink of an eye, he'd cut her throat. She was a mere child of seven years old and he showed no remorse. He was not even satisfied with Hygieia's life; with the place still in darkness, he was answerable to the gods who wanted more. Wanting rid of everything Roman, he hunted the unborn child that *Medica* carried.

'*Medica* was back at the village and she found her father *Cradog;* he'd regained consciousness and asked where Hygieia was. He knew in his heart it was too late to save her and realised as he looked upon *Medica's* face that she too was in danger of being Bran's next victim.

'"I have to send you away, my child, not just for your safety but that of your unborn child, please do as I say," explained *Cradog*. "A friend will guide you to a safe place; under no circumstances are you to return, unless either myself or Cateus come looking for you. If no one comes for you, don't return here because there will be nothing to return to."

'*Medica* was reluctant to leave Hygieia without news of her or me,' Cateus told Dad. 'She knew from what her father had said that she was in danger and her immediate need was to protect our unborn child.

'As foreseen, Bran had gone to look for his next victim, *Medica,* intent on spilling more Roman blood. It was I that angered him the most; I had dared to integrate with his people and he wanted my family destroyed. He was blind with rage and set on destruction of the Romans in order to protect the future of his people. Bran had left for the house of *Medica's* parents.

'Bran stood in the open doorway of *Cradog's* house, clutching his mighty sword. *Cradog* tried to escape his glare. He couldn't understand — he'd known Bran since he was a child… how had this gentle giant of a boy who'd once used his strength to unite his people suddenly changed into a monster intent on killing? He avoided Bran's gaze, knowing that if he lied it would be futile. It had been inevitable that he would come here to look for *Medica. Cradog* found it difficult not revealing her whereabouts from Bran's penetrating mind. If he tried to conceal the evidence, it would only irritate him further and would make the fate of his daughter worse. With no other option, he felt there was only one way out and, as he struggled off the bed where he lay, he threw himself upon Bran's outstretched sword.

'Stood in disbelief, Bran removed his sword from *Cradog's* limp body and gently placed him back onto the bed. "Why?" he asked, stunned.

'"You don't understand. If you hadn't been so blind with rage you would have known for yourself. The child you sacrificed was your own flesh and blood — did you not notice the mark on her hand?" replied *Cradog* as he lay dying. "The girl you killed was *Arianwyn's* granddaughter." *Cradog* sighed deeply, having said enough.

'The words seemed incomprehensible as they fell upon Bran's ears. Instinct drove him to the truth and he returned to the stone. The child remained where he had left her, dead. Bran took her hand gently to see the birthmark and realised the truth *Cradog* had voiced. He fell to his knees in despair, not fully understanding how this was possible. What was happening to his troubled mind? In his thoughts, he believed the child to be his long lost twin sister, Hadean, almost identical in the way she'd looked at the age she'd been when she went missing many years ago. He shook his head, still blaming himself for her disappearance. Suddenly, everything fell into place and reality stared him in the face. Hadean had only five fingers; this child was much like himself and had six fingers on both hands. Wrought with despair at what he'd done, he wished he could undo it.

'Bran was a very powerful druid, and with his many years of experience and knowledge, he could go into the underworld and return unscathed. His intentions this time were not to return; he was willing to undo his destruction by sacrificing himself for the return of Hygieia.

'The ritual began with Bran raising the child in his hands and muttering his incantations to the spirit world, opening the doorway. A strange blue mist gathered around them, encircling them and the sacrificial stone that lay inside the inner ring of standing stones.

'This is what I saw when I arrived,' continued Cateus. 'For news had travelled to me; I too had gone looking for Hygieia and *Medica* at her parent's home. I had found *Cradog* barely alive — his wounds were fatal and I was unable to stop the flow of blood. "What happened? Where's my daughter, where's my beloved Hygieia?" I cried with anguish.

'"I'm sorry, I couldn't do anything to save her — she's dead. Bran has taken her to the Stone of Kings," *Cradog* replied, sobbing weakly.

'"And *Medica*?" I asked.

'"She's gone..." His last breath was unable to finish his sentence, and he passed away in my arms.

'I was left assuming that *Medica* was also dead, that she too had suffered the same fate as my beautiful daughter! As quickly as my legs could carry me, I ran to the stone, where I saw Hygieia. She looked so tiny, her limp, fragile body held in Bran's hands.

'As I neared the stone circle, I saw Bran's sword, standing upright in the ground. Blind with fury as Bran knelt at the sacrificial stone, I entered the inner circle. With all my anger and strength, I picked up the huge weapon and swung it into the air, bringing it down with an almighty blow to the back of his neck — it removed his head clean from his shoulders. The mist that surrounded him had cleared. I retrieved Hygieia, clutching her in my arms, leaving the scene of the severed head, Bran's body still knelt at the stone. Her wound had been quick and fatal; she would not have suffered. I felt helpless and sobbed with grief.'

As Dad looked upon the scene, he also felt the emotion and grief of the situation. The severed head of Bran, his body remaining knelt upright at the stone, was a vision that was hard to remove. Dad watched as he saw Cateus retrieve Hygieia from Bran's hands and take her home to be washed and prepared for cremation. Leaving her body in preparation, Dad saw Cateus return to Bran. Not wanting the sword and its powers to fall into the wrong hands, Cateus wanted to destroy it. When he returned to the scene Bran's body was gone, nowhere to be seen; there was nothing left but the blood-soaked sword.

Cateus carried on with his tale. 'As I took the sword, I felt the strength and power it possessed enter my body and it scared me. It had to be destroyed; its evil had already taken too many lives! I took it to the nearby marshlands and threw it into the depths of the water, offering it to the gods in the hope they would do what was right and return my family safe.

'I returned home with a heavy heart and was confronted by the task of sending Hygieia on her final journey. With the funeral pyre ready, I gave her what had been my payment, the coin from my mother; sadly, it was used to pay her passage to the ferryman. I placed the coin in her mouth and stepped back to light the fire.'

Dad saw him as he stood close by, and felt his pain as he bid his final goodbye. As the flames reached into sky, the sun started to rise. The darkness had finally been lifted after what had felt like many days. Dad then realised where Hygieia's cremation had taken place; it was right where he was standing.

'I spent weeks searching for *Medica* in the surrounding

villages in the hope she was still alive. There was no trace of her and I returned to Gelligaer. With my wife presumed dead and my children also, I requested to return home to see my mother. She was the only family I had left. I was still the only surgeon at the fort and was told that once reinforcements and a replacement were sent from Rome, I could return home.

'The day arrived when the convoy from Rome and supplies were sent. With them came news and I was called to the headquarters. There I was informed of a disaster in Pompeii and Herculaneum. Mount Vesuvius had erupted; there was nothing left of the villages and nothing to return home to. My mother had been killed, along with the rest of her town. I was distraught with grief, unable to take any more torment. There was nothing to live for and I took my own life, hoping to join my family in the spirit world.'

Cateus was cremated at the same spot as Hygieia. Our research of the event in 79 AD, of the eruption of Mount Vesuvius, coincides with the era matched to Cateus' age. The skies were blackened with ash from the volcano, reaching its darkest at Herculaneum at about 4am — the exact time Dad was woken during his dreams— Was it another coincidence?

Dad then asked Cateus, 'Why take your own life?'

'Life without reason has no meaning,' was his reply.

'So what do you want from me? How can I help you?'

A REAL FIND

Summer of 1993.

Our home village of Gelligaer has been populated for over three-and-a-half thousand years. The earliest evidence of this is still visible today — the 'cup marked stone' known as Maen Catwg, along with further evidence of the Bronze Age burial cairns on and around the hillsides of the village.

By 43 AD, the Romans had just begun to invade Britain. During this era, Gelligaer fell under the territory of the Silures and it was their fierce resistance that delayed the Romans in conquering Wales. They suffered many a humiliating defeat at the hands of the Silures, but by 75 AD they had finally taken over, and much of Wales succumbed to Roman control.

There is evidence of two forts built at Gelligaer on the road between Cardiff and Brecon; the first was constructed of earth and timber and garrisoned by auxiliary troops. These auxiliary forts were constructed right across Wales to subdue the native people. The second fort was built alongside the first and more of a permanent structure made of stone. The stonework can still be seen today, although during the Norman Era it was dismantled and the stone recycled to build the Norman Church of today.

Although Dad sometimes travelled as far as Nottingham with the metal detecting club that he belongs to, it was almost six years before he found his first significant find: a small coin.

The coin was found in a field on some farmland that had been searched many times before without any success. In

1993, it had come under development for the new extension of the cemetery at the Norman church of the parish at Gelligaer. When the ground was excavated and the soil transported from one area to another it put the existing land back to the levels visible at the Roman era. The cemetery ground is situated below the site, where remains of the Roman fortress are located and the outline of stonework still visible today.

The small coin turned out to be a Roman silver denarius, with the head of a young prince Nero and dated 33-44 AD. This signified the coin had been struck in the reign of Claudius, Nero's stepfather. Apart from some slight pitting to the surface of the coin, it was in an excellent condition.

The coin was dated and recorded by experts at the National Museum of Wales. It was at the Museum that they suggested the coin had been in a fire or subjected to some kind of heat with the evidence of the pitting — although this has not affected its value and its true beauty remains unspoilt. At the time the condition was not significant; it was truly an exciting find by my father, his first coin from the Roman period.

However, the significance of the date even puzzled the experts. It was, dated much earlier than the Roman occupation of Wales around 60 AD.

CATEUS' STORY: PART 2

'You've received the payment!' exclaimed Cateus, referring to the small, once insignificant coin Dad had found fourteen years ago. 'When I passed over my mother was not there to greet me, therefore she must still be at Herculaneum, waiting for my return as I had promised her. There is a great significance of why you were chosen — the year you were born was 1947…'

Cateus was born in what we know as 47 AD; Dad was born in 1947.

'I've been waiting many, many years for my family to return to this village to help us,' said Cateus.

Cateus implied that he and Dad were of the same bloodline — 'family'. The birthmarks, he explained, were not just coincidence. Dad finding the coin was also fate, and this was the payment Cateus referred to.

Cateus continued with his request. 'I'm unable to leave Gelligaer because this is where Hygieia belongs and she holds me here; she won't let me leave. I will not go without her but I must find my mother. I need your help to reunite me with my mother and it's you that must go to Herculaneum in place of me.'

All three spirits seemed to be stuck in purgatory, unable to move onto the next world, each still waiting to be reunited. Cateus had decapitated Bran, so he also remained in purgatory; he was unable to move on into the next world because he was not a whole being.

Cateus spoke his final words. 'Now you're able to walk in their footsteps… Follow your heart and the rest of the journey will unfold.'

Cateus and Hygieia had disappeared into the ether and Dad was left alone, surrounded by nightfall, back in the cemetery. He was feeling dazed, not knowing where or who he was or how he'd got there. As his eyes adjusted to the evening light, he could make out the surrounding gravestones; there in front of him on the reverse of one such stone in large gold letters, he read the name out loud.

'MALCOLM.'

Dad suddenly came out of what seemed to be a trance, and knew exactly who he was and where. It was like a key word bringing him out of a hypnotic state. The place where the gravestone rested was the very spot Cateus and Hygieia had been cremated, and indeed where he had found the coin. This is why he now believes his parents named him 'Malcolm', and not 'Rees' as his ancestors before him. He felt it was his fate.

On leaving the house, it had been approximately 6:30pm. It was almost 9pm when he returned home, shaken, frightened and totally drained. He was unable to tell his story straight away to my worried mum; he needed to sleep. It was the following day before he explained to my mother what had happened. Initially he was afraid to tell anyone else other than my mum — even me. There was the fear he would be ridiculed because he himself had thought he had 'lost his marbles'. Surely no-one would believe him for a second — he hardly believed it himself!

Dad was left feeling that what had happened was only the middle of the story and there was more to unfold. What would happen next, he wasn't sure.

I believe my dad had a supernatural experience. Spirits with a purpose had visited him and they needed to pass on a message. With the dreams and finding the coin, along with this event, there were too many coincidences to let the story go untold. Had Dad been given the gift, an insight into the past? Quite possibly something had opened his mind and changed his life forever.

How could a trip to Italy reunite these spirits?

Well, we were to embark on a 'family tree' quest that would be the envy of any keen genealogist!

HERCULANEUM

11th August 2007.

After the events at the cemetery, there was a time of difficulty; Dad struggled to come to terms with the supernatural world and to logically comprehend what had happened. Surely, it wasn't possible. It was a time of thought and contemplation — had it been a dream? On the other hand, was his mind playing tricks on him?

Initially he was unable to discuss these events with anyone, except my mother, whom at the time had been worried by his disappearance. She witnessed his return and the state he was in. Dad feared being disbelieved, having once been a sceptic himself.

There was a noticeable change in his manner whilst he contemplated these events. He seemed far away and quieter than usual, and found it difficult at first to express his feelings. It was by accident that I was to hear the story, after walking in on a conversation between Dad and Mum. No longer able to keep it to themselves, family and friends were beginning to become curious and worry about the changes in his nature. Eventually, with the problem shared, his dilemma became easier and the weight on his shoulders had been lifted.

I was in awe and amazed at the detail he described and the story he told. To his astonishment, his family and friends also believed what he told them. The weeks passed by with my dad still unable to shake the event, thinking now of how he would find Cateus' mother, Calla. Should he even consider the journey to Herculaneum? Would it just be a wild goose chase or a journey into the unknown? Then again, what if he'd regret not going — if he didn't make the trip, then what?

By the middle of July, an intense feeling deep inside him grew stronger day by day; there was a sense that this was a journey he had to take. Events still troubled him, as he recalled the quest that was asked of him. There seemed to be some guiding instinct that told him this journey had to be made before the end of August. This was the anniversary date; Mount Vesuvius had erupted on the 24th of August, destroying Pompeii and Herculaneum.

Deep down, from the last event at the cemetery, he knew there was more to the story that he had yet to hear. He had to reunite these lost souls, even though he couldn't be certain the journey would be fruitful.

I can almost hear the sceptics thinking he must be mad to contemplate making such a journey on a whim. To be visited from the spirit world, hard to believe, but to be instructed to perform such a task ludicrous. Being a believer in the spirit world myself and believing in the honesty of my dad, I had a strong determination to go with him. I had a feeling I needed to go with him and be part of this amazing journey. It was only later, whilst in Italy, I realised my father was making this journey with me, his eldest daughter, mirroring Cateus and Hygieia.

By this point Dad was getting used to the idea his experience was meant to be and had actually happened. It wasn't a dream, it couldn't have been a dream, it had physically happened. Once a non-believer himself, now a convert, it had changed his whole perception. Still, those guiding feelings were with him, convincing him he was doing the right thing, as we made our plans to travel to Italy. Preparations were brought forward, what was going to be an October trip now had to take place before the end of August, with something or someone telling him that was the right time.

We arrived in Rome on the 9th of August and settled into our apartment in the heart of the city. The following day was a relaxed trip to the beautiful Vatican City, just around the corner from where we stayed. This then gave us time to plan our journey to Herculaneum, getting our bearings, finding the station and what route options we had — if Herculaneum indeed still existed. Dad was given this name during the time Cateus' mother had lived there. It turned out we were heading towards the modern day village of Portici.

VISIT TO NAPLES AND HERCULANEUM – 'ERCOLANO'

Saturday 11ᵗʰ August 2007.

It was a two-and-a-half-hour train journey from Rome to Naples and we passed the most beautiful countryside along the way. Going through my mind was the task of finding Herculaneum. How would I manage on very little Italian? I was also very aware of the folks back home, worried and anxious. On our arrival to a very busy Naples we saw no sign of Herculaneum on area maps and the language barrier made communication a little difficult to ask. Fortunately, we found the help of a friendly local taxi driver who spoke little English. It was a stroke of luck that, like Pompeii, Herculaneum, or 'Ercolano', was an equally popular tourist site.

We arrived at Herculaneum and the skyline was dominated by the unmistakeable Mount Vesuvius. It was both a grand and scary feature. It is still classed as an active volcano today — but our taxi driver reassured us with a smile on his face, 'It's not working today; it's sleeping.'

It was a strange day full of mixed emotions. Herculaneum had been buried below more than thirty feet of volcanic stone and was almost intact as excavations revealed many objects still whole. We felt a mixture of cold shiver, fear, anxiety and underlying excitement. There were five of us in our party. I was in awe once again of such a wondrous city and insight into the past, a possible place where my ancestors had once lived. If only. The task ahead took priority over sightseeing and I prayed for the adventure to be fruitful.

Dad felt nothing, there was no sense of where he had to

go, the guidance that was once with him had vanished. He only felt a cold shiver pass through his body as he looked upon this once Roman city. Still pondering if he was doing the right thing, part of him feared having to confront yet more ghosts of the past. The feeling came to him once more, leading him in a particular direction, towards the far side of the excavations. Whilst he went off by himself to do what he came here for, the rest of us investigated as tourists.

It was then I matched the map we had to the one that was situated at the site, piecing together the puzzle, discovering Dad was heading to the house of Galba. Yet another coincidence and surprise, this story was a treasure hunt of information. I watched from a distance to see where he walked. I saw him stop, unable to go any further due to a barricade at the end of the street; it was an area under recent excavation. Was this why these events were happening? Had they disturbed evidence, unleashing the spirits? Dad thought he would have to climb over the barrier to get to where he was going — fortunately, there was no need. He was not alone in the street; there were other tourists present.

On nearing the barrier and the house of Galba, everything changed, and as before that same sensation washed over him.

Dad was back in time once again, the street around him now intact and complete, just as it had been in 69 AD. The volcano loomed larger in the background, seemingly doubled in size. He was approached by a female figure coming out of a nearby house to greet him. In his mind, he could hear her call his name — 'Servius?' Not Cateus like Dad had expected. She approached my dad, then stopped and reached out her hand to communicate.

'My name is Calla…' she began.

Without any explanation, through the physical contact alone, she then knew why my dad was there and who had sent him.

Dad was in shock, not knowing what to say or do. Their connection was so strong. The image of Calla was like looking at a picture of his grandmother, Violet; they were almost identical. Violet's dark hair and Calla's fair hair was the only difference. One of the first things he noticed was the identical birthmark on her hand, like Violet's and Hygieia's.

The vision and surroundings then changed to another time; Calla was now showing Dad slaves bound together. Lined up against an outside wall were men, women and children of different races and sizes, all dressed in ragged clothes. Dad was stood behind a man dressed in a white robe, edged with a red and gold band around the sleeves and a diagonal sash of the same colour. The Roman figure before him viewed the slaves on display, stopping at a small, fair-haired girl. She was dirty and her hair was badly tangled. Her eyes were focused on the ground as he approached her and placed his finger beneath her chin, lifting her head to see her piercing blue eyes. One look into those eyes and his choice was made; he took hold of her hand gently and they walked away together.

The vision was of Calla; she had been only a child when she was torn from her homeland. The shock was unbearable and she refused or was unable to speak for many months. It was her new master that had given her the name 'Calla'.

Dad was now taken back to the vision of the street where they'd met, and there was a taste of sulphur in his mouth. What looked like great piles of smoke swept down the mountainside and he felt he was being choked. The volcano was erupting. Calla was running for her life. She carried something under her arm but it was too difficult to see what it was. Dad also sensed himself running with her. Looking back, they both saw the thick black clouds of dust rolling towards them. Then complete darkness. Feeling the fear within Calla, they both had to escape — quickly. Heading for a way out towards the sea, the terror felt so real!

Villa of Galba, at Herculaneum.

Suddenly he was back in the street, outside Galba's house. Everything was back to normal, except spiritually he was not alone; Calla had bonded with him and wanted to return home with him and to her son, Cateus. Feeling the need to get out, and still fearing the sight of the volcano, he came looking for us and met with me first.

I had never seen Dad so emotional. He took a moment to catch his breath. 'It was like seeing my grandmother, Violet; they looked so alike,' he told me, quite choked by the experience and her presence.

We were all blown away by his experience and the story he told. There is no doubt he had an ability to be taken into the past through the medium of these spirits. We were relieved our journey had been fruitful and had put an end to the negative thoughts of doubt. We now knew he had done the right thing!

Mount Vesuvius, view from Herculaneum.

The boat houses at Herculaneum, where most bodies were found. They had been attempting to escape.

Street view leading to Galba's villa.

VISIT TO THE COLISEUM AND PALATINE HILL

Sunday 12ᵗʰ August 2007.

The next day we visited the Coliseum. We were strangers in a foreign land. Well, all of us but Dad; he didn't feel like a stranger, he felt as though he'd walked there before. Of course, he hadn't; it was his first visit to Rome. Was it the presence of Calla that made him feel this way?

Whilst at the Coliseum, the foreground of Palatine Hill, he knew with her presence this was also a place he had to be. It was little wonder with Calla with him that he didn't feel like a stranger. He could also feel the presence of Galba. Rome was once home to them; this was where they would have been entertained during his time as Emperor.

Palatine Hill was a climb, not a walk, and the very steep slope had many, many steps before we reached the top. As we explored, Dad felt so at home that he said walking there was as familiar as walking around his own garden.

The heat of the day had been almost unbearable. Dad told us that here at the forum was where Galba was executed. Becoming very emotional once again, he described his and Calla's mixed feelings of happiness and sadness. Calla was glad he had brought her here to revive the happy memories of what was once her home, but their sadness stemmed from bidding farewell to the place that she had been content. She was also saying goodbye to Rome and to the memory of Galba, knowing she would never return. This was what Dad could not understand: if Rome was her home and where she had been happiest, then why was she so willing to leave it all behind? He felt there must be another reason why she was coming back to Gelligaer, other than to be reunited with Cateus and meet her granddaughter.

VISIONS OF THE PAST

August 2008 – January 2009.

On our return from Italy, we felt as though our journey of mixed emotions had been most worthwhile. Dad was eager now to return to the cemetery and to the spot where he had met with Cateus in the hope to reunite him with the present spirit of his mother, Calla.

His initial visit back presented nothing, there was no presence of Cateus, no visions or changes in environment. Rather disappointed, he returned home. Two or three weeks passed by with the usual visits to the cemetery and still nothing, even when he took those visits by himself.

He asked himself why Calla was still with him. Why didn't she seem in a hurry to leave and return to Cateus?

Maybe like the other occurrences the time just wasn't right and he would have to wait, hoping that Calla would show him the way.

Some weeks later and he still wondered what the point of his trip to Italy had resolved. Why had there been no further contact from Cateus? He'd seemed so eager to be reunited with his mother and for Dad to make the trip. Dad wished for something to happen, if only to release the spirit of Calla from her limbo; she was constantly by his side. He had no choice but to put her presence to the back of his mind, to get on with day-to-day living and not dwell on the thoughts of the trip to Herculaneum.

Knowing that when the time was right events would unfold naturally, he began to relax. It was when he was more at ease with the situation, relaxed and alone, that the daydreams started to occur. Random visions occurred as he went about his day, confusing and conflicting with the evidence of what he'd already seen. He tried to avoid them at first by keeping himself busy and finding extra jobs to do. Was this Calla's doing? Was she presenting him with the images? Was there a reason for her not wanting to leave — perhaps she had unfinished stories she wanted to tell.

The first vision was of the Druid Dad now knew as Bran. Conflicted evidence to what he'd seen previously, Bran was being nailed to a cross by Roman soldiers. How could that be possible? Dad was confused, having already seen him beheaded and killed by Cateus! This image was presented several times over a number of days. Bran being crucified and left to die on the cross puzzled him; how could he have been crucified when he was already slain by his own sword at the hand of Cateus?

A different vision was equally strange: a giant of a man from a different era to Bran and the Roman Cateus. His clothing much more basic, made from animal skin, with shoulder length hair. He had a young, boyish face with no facial hair. Strapped to his back, he carried a stone pillar as large as himself. It was lifted a little way from the ground and appeared a foot or two above his shoulder height. The immense weight of the stone gave him cause to walk with a stoop. He obviously belonged to a much earlier period in time; what was his connection to the story?

Another vision was of twin stone pillars, about nine feet in height, standing a few metres apart. Both stones were identical in shape and size. Playing around the stones were what appeared to be two men. Dressed in animal skins, they played like children. It was only when they turned around and Dad was able to see their faces that it was obvious they were children; young and fresh-faced boys. They were identical in every way, signifying they must be twins. He immediately felt these twin boys must have a strong connection to the twin pillars.

Strongly indicated was the feeling these stone pillars stand where the Druids once lived. Dad therefore associated them with Anglesey. Thus began our research of the Druids and Anglesey. It was a book from the library that led us to the discovery of the twin stones, as Dad had described. On showing him the picture we'd found, it was obvious from his face these were the stones seen in his vision; even the surrounding landscape was identical. They were the twin stones at Penrhos Feilw, Anglesey.

Still came further daytime visions; the next one an aerial view of land. Close to the coast was a huge lake with a strip of land separating it from the coast. Dad felt a certain familiarity about the place; this was home to the ancestors of the Druids and the twin boys he'd seen previously. It was an island across the sea from Anglesey; it must be Ireland, Dad thought. Reaching for the Atlas, it was indeed the same shape and the area where the strip of land was seen, identical to that of Northern Ireland near Belfast.

These visions were all connected somehow, and had links to the missing parts of the story that Dad felt had yet to be told. Were they visions of the past or mere glimpses of things yet to happen?

The most prominent vision was that of the man who carried the stone. Another vision confirmed Dad's suspicions that he was one of the twin boys seen previously. Looking more of a man, he still possessed the face of a young boy and continued to carry the stone. As an adult he stood at least seven feet tall, and was followed by a heavily pregnant woman of average height. There seemed to be no sign of the other twin; again the connection was strong between the boys and the twin stones. It was as if they were placed there to commemorate their birth, Dad felt.

Dad's day was continually interrupted by these visions, and it appeared to be affecting his thoughts, making him appear far away and distant at times.

Recalling the day he spoke to Cateus, Dad suddenly remembered his final words, remembered what he'd been told to do...

'To walk in their footsteps'.

His sudden eureka moment reminded him of Cateus'

request; he realised this was surely the reason Calla was still with him — she was leading the way to the next events. With all this information mulling around in his head, visions still appeared, and he decided where best to start. He knew he must retrace their footsteps; where else would be better to begin than that of Gelligaer, his home village? Using his instincts and that of Calla's spirit for guidance, he knew of one of the oldest landmarks, a large stone, simply known to him as 'the cup stone'. Although aware of its existence, he only had a vague idea where it was, having never been there before. He hoped for the best in finding it. In over thirty years of living in Gelligaer, this would be his first visit to Maen Catwg.

He was dubious and anxious of what might happen, but at least he had the opportunity to inform my mum this time of where he was going.

Arriving with the guidance of Calla to the field of this ancient landmark, he could see the large stone slab from some distance away. Other than Calla, he was on his own, but now had the strange feeling of many others present and was far from alone. He walked around the field first, picking up the presence of people working and living in close proximity in what once seemed a large settlement. Clear images now appeared of these people, and he was able to identify that there were once two tribes, living in harmony; some stood seven feet tall and some were of more average height, standing at about five foot.

Still anxious to approach the stone, he took a walk over to the far side of the field. A different sensation was felt there, a cold feeling of death. He was walking in the presence of where they buried their dead. The settlement of these people had been here for a long period; they seemed happy and content with their surroundings.

With trepidation, the stone drew him closer; the unknown and previous events filled him with fear, making him afraid to touch it at first. The lack of contact with these images or spirits around him meant that it felt very much like watching a silent movie. On closer inspection of the stone, the number of cup marks and its overall size amazed him. It was long and fairly wide, about a foot in height and flat. At one end in a circular pattern lay the cup indentations, some large and clear, others smaller and more weathered.

Seizing the moment, he touched its side. Although the day was bitterly cold, the stone felt warm; there was a sensation of a heartbeat felt within. It seemed obvious to Dad that the largest hole would have been the last to be placed there, and so he placed his hand upon it. The presence of Bran and the appearance of his familiar face was shown before him. No longer frightened, he tried some others and found that each cup mark presented the appearance of a face, some unfamiliar, some familiar. The face of Hygieia, Cateus' daughter, was among them. The least visible cup mark, what seemed the oldest, evoked the face of the young twin, the one that had carried a stone pillar. Each cup represented an individual and all were connected.

This was the very stone Hygieia had been sacrificed upon. Looking up at the surrounding landscape and being in contact, with the stone acting as the channel, he realised the stone had been moved. Its original place had been on the brow of a hill, similar to the hill where today's church stands, surrounded by a circle of standing stones. The surrounding stones are of irregular shapes, but are all tall and upright, with the cup stone at the centre.

It appeared to be a small henge, a place of worship and sacrifice.

Maen Catwg is described in the history books as a capstone to a burial or that of rock art. However, like many stones it does have an air of mystery. Many of the marks are very faint due to weathering. Some are still large, suggesting these marks had been made later. In theory, surely, if it were rock art, the marks would appear to have been made at the same time!

Dad was still touching the stone. The stone provided the images and revealed its purpose. It seemed to be a sacrificial stone, or a death stone. It was used by Bran to sacrifice Hygieia, but it was also where they placed their dead. The cups were collecting receptacles for the blood, and a gateway for the rulers of the Silures and their ancestors before. When dead upon the stone, their spirit and life force would be absorbed, received into the earth via the stone, to their underworld, their heaven, and into the next life. Each king upon coronation would make their own cup mark, ready for the time when they came to depart their life. This would in theory explain the difference in timescale of the cup marks.

Moving away from that vision, Dad then moved back to the view of the settlement field, still in contact with the stone. Approaching the stone was the huge man who carried the stone pillar, closely shadowed by the heavily pregnant woman, who followed out of loyalty. Behind her was a whole tribe of people, between a hundred to two hundred followers; they were clearly an amalgamation of two tribes.

Dad had been gone for some time when his connection was interrupted. Returning to the present time, the strange vision of the sun and moon appeared close together, something he'd never seen before.

He was now convinced that this was what Cateus meant by 'walk in their footsteps'; the village itself held the key. Were there more footprints, stories or secrets to uncover? This was undoubtedly a place where they had walked, leaving their visible landmarks and footsteps behind, like carbon printing.

A TWIN'S LIFE

December 2007.
Era 2,500 BC.

It was almost four months since our visit to Herculaneum and there was still no sign of fulfilment from the task Cateus had asked of Dad. There had only been visions during the daytime of what seemed like the next link, events of the story yet to unfold.

It was just before Christmas. I was leaving my new home at Deri when Dad decided to take the mountain route home to Gelligaer. Along the route he approached the junction in the road; stood there beside the road was the twin, carrying his stone. Unlike the other visions, this was an actual sighting of a physical presence. The twin seemed to have been waiting, and although he was some distance away it was clear to see he was a giant of a man. With his hands held up by his head, he carried a heavy burden. After a short wait, he continued his walk across the field.

Dad stopped the car, thinking he had imagined the apparition. He got out of the car and began to follow him, but it was like chasing the end of a rainbow. No matter how fast or slow he walked, the same distance remained between them. The twin walked through the fence as if it were invisible; Dad had to climb over it in order to follow him. The distance between him and the car was getting greater and, not knowing where he was being led, he became concerned. Deciding not to continue, he went home instead.

Was his imagination getting the better of him? What was it he saw, a vision or a spirit? Where was he going?

It was after Christmas on a wet and miserable day that Dad saw the twin again. He waited in the same place as before. Due to the weather, Dad stayed in the car, parking up and watching him until he walked out of sight. He kept looking back with beckoning glances, wanting eagerly to be followed.

The twin was the next link, he had to be. Dad knew it was another sign and knew he would have to follow him.

To walk in their footsteps.

And so, he waited for a dry day and donned a good pair of walking boots. Although very nervous, he was prepared and anticipated another journey back in time. Dad left the car at home this time, hoping he was doing the right thing. When he approached the wall there stood the twin, waiting in the same spot as before. He waited for Dad to approach and then, before he got too close, he began to walk away. Dad followed and no matter how hard he tried to catch up, to be directly behind him, it was just not possible.

The twin carried his heavy burden, not stopping for a moment's rest. In the blink of an eye, it happened as before. The scenery had not changed but the colour and texture of the picture had, Dad knew he was walking back in time. The surrounding farmland was unchanged in the era he was walking into. But It felt different and was definitely a time before Bran and Cateus. Judging by his clothing and the area becoming more and more desolate, it seemed more primitive to the time in which they had lived.

Their walk continued over open ground, surrounded by woodland, different to the segregated farmland in today's era. The familiarity of the landscape told Dad they were headed towards where the Norman church and the Roman fort remains lie today. This confirmed his suspicion of an earlier era, as no presence of either building existed in this journey. Dad continued to follow, and then the ghostly figure stopped and disappeared.

Confused and stuck in this time zone, Dad was now alone. It was not too long before a great many more people joined him, all dressed in a primitive way. Having no contact with these apparitions or spirits meant it was just as if he was watching a silent movie again, with not a single sound to be heard. He watched as they walked on, showing the journey they had undertaken. It had been a lengthy voyage, from Anglesey to Gelligaer. He felt their anger, frustration and tiredness; many have suffered along the way. All the feelings and places rushed through Dad's mind; he needed no words or explanation.

It was clear their journey had begun many moons ago, with the two boys playing around the twin stones at Penrhos Feilw, which can be found at Anglesey today. The elder twin was clearly the more dominant character and he pursued the younger into some sort of mock hunting game. Identical in every way physically, they were like one being with a split personality.

The first-born twin was typically boyish, filled with wild devilment, born under the eyes of the moon. Amongst many of their beliefs this was a bad omen; the sun and moon were worshipped highly. Therefore, he was given the name of the moon deity: *Llune.*

Born under the eyes of the rising sun was the second child; a good omen. He was given the name of the sun deity: *Llugh.* By nature, he was quiet and shy.

Dad was not told the twins' names, only that they were named after the deities under which they were born; this information was shown to him through symbolism. It was also an era where the spoken word was not written nor indeed did they have any of the knowledge or understanding we have today. In our own research, we gave the boys these names in accordance to the symbols being shown.

Back on the Island of Anglesey, where they lived, were two tribes that each kept themselves to themselves. One tribe stood very tall, almost seven foot in height, to which *Llune* and *Llugh* belonged. These were people who'd travelled from across the sea, from the land that is now called Ireland.

The other race was of average height and native to Anglesey at that time. They lived separately and in fear of one another, each aware of the other's existence but kept apart by the unknown. They remained within their own boundaries.

Whilst out on a hunt one day, they carried with them their large bows, arrows and spears. *Llune,* the more dominant twin, wanted to be daring and venture to the other side of the island. He knew it was forbidden by his father, and it was just for mere devilment he urged *Llugh* to follow. *Llugh* was not so eager; his honest and true nature didn't permit him to disobey his father's word. They picked up the tracks of some kind of wild boar and began to hunt it down. In the distance they heard the cry of wolves; it sounded like they had just captured their prey. The boys saw stealing what the wolves had captured as an easier challenge than stalking the boar. Changing direction, they headed off towards the cries of the wolves.

With the wolves now in sight, they could see no sign of a wounded animal, but it seemed as if they had something trapped up a tree. On closer inspection, it appeared to be a person. *Llune* was disappointed and not bothered by the distress of the trapped individual; he wanted to go back to hunting the boar. *Llugh,* with his kind heart, wanted to help the trapped person. As he got nearer he could see it was a young girl, from the other side of the island. *Llugh* had the difficult task of persuading his brother for help. Eventually giving in to his brother's persuasion, *Llune* helped chase off the wolves, making loud noises and throwing stones. However, what was more difficult was persuading the young girl to come out of the tree.

She was more afraid of them than the wolves, having never seen such beings before and only hearing of them in stories. They were giants compared to her, a strange sight indeed. With his friendly charm, it was *Llugh* who coaxed her down by offering her food. Realising they meant her no harm, she was grateful to the strangers who'd saved her from the pack of hungry wolves. Both boys agreed to return her safely back to her own village. They were fascinated by her beauty; her attraction was so overwhelming they neglected their skills as hunters and had no idea they were being followed. Before they had reached her village, her people bearing arms ambushed them; they'd assumed the boys held her captive. Immediately on the defensive, the twins made ready with their own weapons.

Outnumbered, the girl spoke out first. She defended the boys, telling her father they had saved her. Their weapons were dropped to show their gratitude. Still intrigued by the girl, they returned to the village with her people.

Having struck a bond with the people, it was the girl named *Siwan* that now intrigued them. Her attraction made them regular visitors and their bond soon blossomed into friendship. Their regular presence and familiarity meant they were no longer feared as a race. They no longer felt threatened, as they learned the tribe was a peaceful one and meant no harm. Leading the way forward, it was the twins who felt confident it was time to approach each other as a tribe. It was not long before they began to mix, trading goods and knowledge. In time, they had built up their trust, becoming closer as a community. Amalgamation was inevitable.

The twins shared a really strong bond and had a close relationship that made them inseparable. Adolescence was fast approaching and both were aware of the effect and hold their new female friend *Siwan* now had over them. It was as if they were under a spell and it was much more than a friendship: both boys had fallen in love. Each of them was not aware of the other's feelings toward *Siwan*. This was bound to cause problems. She too had begun to form a special friendship with the boys; romantically her feelings lay with *Llugh*, understandably the gentler of the two.

Meanwhile the newly combined tribe were reaching a dilemma. King *Miah*, the twins' father, was old and frail and was required to choose his successor. Obviously the usual method of natural selection, father to son, was not so easy with twin boys.

Miah remembers the difficulties in conceiving an heir and how delighted they had been to be blessed with two sons, each one a precious gift. Both boys were equally suited to be a leader of people in their father's eyes. *Llune*, being slightly older, believed it was his duty to succeed his father. *Miah* found it a difficult choice to make by himself and required some help.

He chose to seek advice from the leader of the other tribe, *Siwan's* father. His suggestion was that the successor, whoever was chosen, would quite simply take his daughter as their wife. This decision caused friction amongst the twins.

Llugh quite simply was not interested in becoming king; his only interest was marriage to *Siwan,* whom he loved dearly. Knowing that he could not have one without the other left him frustrated. Tension grew between the boys, as *Llune* wanted the kingdom more than anything, but would also like to take *Siwan* as his wife. It was *Llune* who continually pressed his father for a decision, believing he'd be the chosen one. This pestering made the dilemma a constant battle of conscience and a reminder of how imminent his decision was to be.

King *Miah* had to seek further advice from the 'elderly shaman', *Gwyddium*, whose advice was to ask the gods for their decision. *Gwyddium* took the King to the gateway, the standing stones (at Penrhos Feilw). As they arrived, the sky was filled by the sun and moon; it was midday and they were unusually close together. Both men looked upon this as strange; the sun and moon seemed to be getting closer before their eyes and they feared a collision; an event that was to occur in their unwritten history, a tale to be foretold and passed on from generation to generation. Fearing the gods were angry with them, *Gwyddium* set about sacrificing a young goat as a truce in return for their guidance.

They stepped up to the stones, which were poignant to *Miah* because he'd placed them there to commemorate the birth of his sons, as well as being their gateway to a new land and a new beginning. Stood very still, they watched the moon devour the sun and believed it to be a bad omen. The message told that *Llune* would defeat his brother. With the sun now consumed the land was plunged into darkness. Drawing his sword with anger at the gods for their prediction, the King hurled it toward the sky in the hope they accept its power and spare his son's life. Slowly the sun began to emerge out of the darkness; the first beam of light fell down upon the sword, now stood upright in the ground between the stones as if placed there. The sun and moon parted and normal daylight resumed, the sword was surrounded by an ethereal glow.

Taking hold of the sword, *Miah* tried to retrieve it from the ground but was unable to move it. It remained steadfast. He turned to the wise old shaman for an answer and was met by a vacant expression; the shaman appeared to be in a trance.

He uttered the words, 'The gods have set their task; whoever is able to draw the sword will be the true and rightful heir.' Snapping out of the trance and regaining his composure, *Gwyddium* was totally unaware of his words. He looked upon King *Miah's* face as if he'd seen a ghost.

The sword remained in the ground. Dad felt the enormity of its power and emotion that surrounded it. It truly was a magnificent object fit for a king. As it was stuck there in the ground, there was an air of mystery to how it got there — it was unmoveable! How did it hold so much power?

With the task now set, its preparations were put in motion immediately. Time was running out for the King. There was to be a huge celebration and a gathering of many. The twins were prepared for the event, each wanting victory.

The night before the ceremony *Llune* hatched a devious plan: he tricked the soon-to-be-betrothed *Siwan* into sleeping with him, but not as himself; by pretence he played the convincing role of his brother *Llugh*. With his identical looks and his falsely adopted sweet nature, she was totally fooled.

The celebration was quite an event — a ceremony of new beginnings. Both tribes had gathered around the stones to witness the event, and there was much excitement amongst the crowds. The arrival of the twins and King *Miah* created a ripple of eagerness. *Llune* insisted on the first attempt; he thought that, being the strongest, the kingdom would surely be his. He stepped up to the challenge and with all his might tried to remove the sword from the ground. Unmoveable as the sword seemed, he would not give up until his arms ached so badly that he was forced to stop from the pain.

Next in line was *Llugh*. As he approached the sword it began to shine brightly, and still glowed as he took it in his hands. With very little effort, it eased itself out of the ground. There was great joy and happiness amongst the people as they cheered for the victor. The King himself was elated, and he collapsed to the ground a happy man; with the rightful heir in place it was time to move on for him. *Llugh* caught sight of his father's demise and dropped the sword to run to his aid. As he did so, his brother was intent on retrieving the sword for a second time. Still illuminated, it lay on the ground as he grabbed hold. It burnt his hands and he released his grip immediately, dropping it to the ground. He fled from the scene and disappeared from sight.

With the King dead and a new ruler in place, there was a period of respect and mourning before the marriage could take place. *Llugh's* sadness in losing his father was compensated by his happiness and success to marry his true love. It was within this period of mourning that *Siwan* found she was pregnant. Of course, she assumed the father of the child to be her husband-to-be and had no worry in telling *Llugh* the good news. When *Siwan* broke the news it was plain to see it was a surprise to *Llugh*. He was shocked, and knew it could only be down to one other... his brother. She was fearful that *Llugh* would no longer want to marry her, but he eased her concern.

'It makes no difference to me that the child belongs to my brother,' he said reassuringly.

Llugh felt the child was equally his, being of the same flesh and blood, and so it would be treated as if his own.

Angered, *Llune* returned to the village, wanting to claim what was rightfully his: the kingdom. He presented a challenge to fight his brother, but *Llugh* refused. It was not in his nature to fight, especially not against his own kin. Even though the sword gave him enormous strength and an indestructible power, he would not use it against his own flesh and blood.

Llugh attempted to welcome him back in peace, to no avail. There was no hope of reconciliation and, turning his back, *Llugh* walked away. Seizing the opportunity, *Llune* cowardly prepared to strike his brother in the back. Just as he was about to, *Siwan* appeared in the doorway; she called out to warn *Llugh* of the danger. *Llugh* drew his sword and faced his brother to defend himself. *Llune* charged towards his brother and fell onto the outstretched sword. The look of disbelief and horror was clear on both of their faces.

Grief-stricken at the tragedy, *Llugh* took his brother in his arms. *Llugh* told him how sorry he was as he lay dying. He told him that he knew about *Siwan* and the fact that the child she carried was his. *Llugh* promised his brother that, whether the child be a boy or girl, it would be the next heir and the next leader of their people.

Llune was happy with that thought and made his peace before dying in his brother's arms.

Nothing could ease *Llugh's* pain as he prepared his brother's body for cremation. *Llugh* washed and bathed his brother's wound and decided to stay the night with him. He didn't want him to be left alone. He fell asleep on his brother's chest and in his dreams that night their father *Miah* appeared. The King told *Llugh* that the sword would no longer be his power, as it had taken his own blood. It had to be cleansed, for it would no longer serve him, and it had to be returned from whence it came, from between the stones.

King *Miah* went on to predict that if he failed to return the sword, the land would be cursed and no longer yield good crops. There would be nothing here for him or his people, but he warned him to leave the next day and take his brother — 'For he will show the way.'

Llugh awoke from his strange dream and felt the hardness of something cold beneath his cheek. With his eyes wide open he looked at where his brother lay; his body had gone, to be replaced with a large stone pillar the size of his body. Remembering his dream and his father's words, he didn't go looking for the body. He hadn't moved all night, so assumed the stone to be his brother.

Firstly, he took the sword with his father's closest friend, the shaman, to return it to the stones as requested. *Gwyddium* told the twin he would stay as guardian of the sword until it was needed again by his people. This meant he would remain on the island in isolation whilst the new amalgamated tribe left and found a new land in which to prosper.

Taking command of his people, the young *Llugh* strapped his stone brother to his back. He allowed no one to help him with his struggle. He felt it was his penance, given to him by his father. Ready, he began the journey with his people following as one, with their worldly possessions and livestock.

This solved the mystery as to why Dad had seen both average height people and those he regarded as giants travelling and living as one unit.

Immediately behind the twin, and the only person who seemed willing to help him, was his heavily pregnant wife, *Siwan*. They had begun their journey from Anglesey to make a new home, wherever that was to be. Each evening they set up camp for the night, and the following day the stone brother would point the way to continue their journey. Many days and nights passed; the longer and further they travelled, the more the followers grew weary, restless to settle. There had been many an opportunity along the way and they had seen no reason to go any further — they were tired of this endless trek. Loyalty for their leader was the only reason they continued but they were anxious to know where he was taking them and what his own reasons to continue were.

Each day they travelled less as the twin grew tired and weak. The straps holding the stone now cut into his shoulders, leaving deep, bleeding welts. Still he made no fuss.

It was then that Dad appeared to be seeing familiar surroundings. They were at the brow of a hill, and had reached Gelligaer — close to where previous events had taken him.

Pausing for a moment, it seemed the twin's strength was about to give up and he fell to his knees. Weary and so tired, he hadn't the strength to release the stone from his back. His followers stood and watched, not wanting him to get up and continue their journey. They hoped this would be the end, so no help was given to him. It was *Siwan,* heavily pregnant, who urged them to help; she struggled to release the burden. Collapsing with the onset of labour pains, she was hurried away by the women who rushed to her aid. Kneeling on the floor in pain, she reached out to her husband, distraught that she was unable to help him. When she was out of sight his straps were cut, releasing the stone. He collapsed on the ground, unconscious, and they left him there.

'The cup stone', Maen Catwg, Gelligaer.

Malcolm Jones.

After releasing the straps, the men took possession of the stone and rolled it down the hillside, where it stopped at the bottom. No one had much cared for the *Llugh*, and he was left where he lay for several hours. As night fell, they began to tend his body and assumed he was dead. He was prepared and laid out on a nearby stone (the 'cup stone', Maen Catwg), a large flat slab of rock ideal and fit for the purpose.

Dad was now stood where the 'cup stone' lies today, after following the twin. The vision projected to him showed that this wasn't its original place. Its surroundings suggested it lay nearer to where the church now stands.

Llugh was laid out, presumed dead. The following day, as the sun rose over the brow of the hill, the light it cast on the ground travelled towards the stone. It reached the stone and continued to cover *Llugh's* body with its warm glow.

As if by some act of the gods, particularly the sun god, from whom *Llugh* received his name, he sat bolt upright and got to his feet. He had been awoken from the dead, as though death was merely sleep. With his strength regained, his immediate thought was that of his task and his brother. He was wearing rough animal skin trousers with a waistcoat-type top of similar fur. The rope welts around his shoulders were clearly visible as he searched the area for the stone pillar.

Appearing from the nearby camp, *Siwan* approached him. In her arms she held the newborn boy. She was not as surprised to see him as the others were. She had not been told that he had been dead, therefore his miraculous recovery did not shock her. Both of them frantically searched for his stone brother, who had vanished from the spot where he'd been abandoned. They were unable to find him.

Llugh took hold of the baby and neared the edge of the hillside to take a look down. There, firmly planted in the ground, stood his stone brother. Almost running down the hillside, they stood before him, the sun falling on the face of his brother. So proudly he stood, surrounded by long grass and wild flowers that grew two-foot high around the base. There were no visible signs of flattened grass from the statue rolling down the hillside; it was as if it'd always been there.

Llugh held the baby boy up to the stone, showing his brother with delight, telling him that he would keep the promise he had made that his son would be the next king. He realised this was where they were meant to stay. It was the resting place of his stone brother, signifying the end of his task. The birth of the child confirmed this, and was seen as a good omen despite him being born at night like his father — thus earning the name *Llune*. They had travelled to Gelligaer and settled.

BRAN'S FAMILY

12ᵗʰ January 2008.
The beginning of a new century AD.

Further feelings urged Dad to take another walk, and again he was guided to the 'cup stone'. The stone for him had a strong presence and was of great significance to these people — both to the twins and that of Bran's family.

He walked straight into the past as he reached the stone; this time it was the beginning of a new century. Dad had walked into family life. Bran was a mere child with the body of a man. He was very different to his twin sister Hadean, who was much smaller in size. Life at home looked basic. He lived with his father Etah, his elder brother Legge and his twin sister, Hadean. Because of his size Bran seemed much older than his years, and was treated so. There was no mother figure present, and this posed a question: had she died in childbirth?

It was a time of unrest in the village, and in the surrounding villages. There was conflict between villages and their chieftains; all were competing for the big prize of total power. There were many raids taking place and livestock were being stolen from the other tribes that were all part of the Silures.

The Silures were widespread across the region, but the conflicts between them were caused by the chieftains of the villages. Etah was the King of the Silures and his title would be passed on to a son, or whoever was next in line. In time and with natural dispersion, descendants left to create their own settlement. Each sibling in turn branched off to create more villages down the line, so each village being in control would in effect be related to the next. Etah's village was getting smaller. Depleted numbers hampered his overall control. Etah held his power in Gelligaer, but his strength and bravery were not enough to control them all as one community. He didn't know how to create peace so they could be brought together as one harmonious tribe.

As a child, Etah was told a story, as I'm sure his father and his father before him would have shared, about a sword. A sword that would give complete power and strength to whoever possessed it. He was curious and wanted to visit Anglesey, the birthplace of the story, to see if the legend was true. He took his eldest son Legge with him, leaving the twins Bran and Hadean under the protection and care of the village. Bran was not happy about this, as he was eager to travel with his father and brother. Etah convinced Bran that he was being left in a position of great responsibility, charged with the task of looking after his sister and being the man of the house. Bran stayed, realising the importance of the job, but was reluctant to not be going with them.

Etah and Legge left promptly, knowing there was a special day they had to be in Anglesey: the festival of the summer solstice. When they reached the island, they were met by hundreds of people from all over Wales. A huge feast was set out and people were eating, drinking and celebrating the forthcoming solstice.

According to the story, the sword would appear with the rising of the sun. When the sun cleared the horizon completely, if the chosen one was on the island the sword would remain in sight for any contenders to remove from the ground. If the chosen one was not on the island, the sword would disappear.

Before sunset, there were seven challengers for the task, including Etah and Legge. They were called to the guardian of the sword, the seven-foot-tall Druid that was left on the island in the days of the twins *Llune and Llugh*, which was some 2,000 years ago.

Dad was confused about how it was possible — how

could this be the same man? No one can survive that long... it was impossible, but he was certain it was the same face as he'd seen before.

The Druid wanted to see their hands. He stood head and shoulders above them all. He inspected Etah's hands first, then Etah noticed the Druids hands. He had six fingers on each hand; Etah was confused and curious. He told the Druid of his own son, Bran, who also had six fingers on each hand. 'He's also of unusual size, like yourself,' he said in wonder.

'I would very much like to meet him,' replied the Druid. He was disappointed to hear that Etah hadn't brought him along.

As the sun rose over the horizon, the sword appeared briefly. The sun cleared the horizon but the sword disappeared, indicating the chosen one was not present on the island. All seven contenders were left bemused.

Suddenly, Dad was taken back to the vision of home life with Bran and Hadean.

Bran was looking for his sister. One of the villagers told him they'd seen her down by the stream, playing with the other children. Setting off, he found her happily throwing stones in the water.

Dad felt Bran's anger and pain of the event. As the children played happily by the stream, a man on a white stallion appeared, instilling fear in the older children who fled, hiding amongst the bushes. Hadean was left by the stream in the open; she was scooped up by the horseman and kidnapped.

Bran witnessed the event from a distance as he approached the stream, but was unable to do anything. Running after them, he shouted his sister's name continually until he was exhausted and unable to run any further. Returning to the village, he was weak and filled with great sadness. Telling the men folk what had happened, they too set out to search for her on horseback. They returned sometime later with no sign of his sister, Hadean.

Bran grew ever more worried and fearful of his father's

return, conscious of his failed attempt to look after his beloved sister. He'd let his father down, and even worst he'd failed his sister, whom he feared he would never see again.

Etah returned to the village and was met on the outskirts by some of his men who proceeded to tell him of his daughter, the deep sadness and anxious await felt by Bran. Bran expected him to be angry, but his father was far from that, he blamed himself more than he blamed his son for Hadean's kidnapping. He was equally upset over her loss and comforted Bran, telling him how proud he was of him for doing everything he could and the bravery that he showed. He reassured him that he wasn't to blame.

Etah, Legge and Bran set out on horseback, riding through all the neighbouring villages in search of Hadean. They found themselves questioning the villagers in the hope that someone might have heard of her whereabouts. They were gone for many a day and night before returning to the village in dismay.

Etah was deeply saddened by the loss of his daughter; it had affected his whole wellbeing. He'd lost all purpose in life without Hadean. He was left feeling weak and vulnerable, and the neighbouring Silures decided to take advantage of his situation and prepared to challenge his leadership. One of his own loyal men informed him of the situation, and of the approaching village bearing arms.

Much tension was felt between both villages as they met, and a skirmish seemed inevitable.

During the battle that commenced Etah was badly wounded by the opposing chieftain and needed urgent treatment. Knowing his wound to be fatal, he pleaded with his son Legge; he was worried about further retaliations; he did not think they could cope. The other tribes would soon join forces, pushing harder for defeat whilst their tribe was weakened even further. He begged Legge to take Bran to Anglesey, where the Druid would take care of them. They would be safe there. Both boys were not keen to leave their father to die; they wanted to stay and fight with him. After much pleading, Legge unwillingly accepted his father's request and promised to take his brother to safety.

There seemed no time, as Etah was informed of more advancing tribes, very close by. He urged Legge to help him to his feet, and to Bran to fetch his sword and shield.

'It is time, boys — you must go — quickly.'

The boys did as they were told, urgently heading for Anglesey. Etah prepared to do all he could to defend his village with his loyal tribe, to hold them off until they were safely out of harm's way. Once at a safe distance, the boys looked back and saw the smoke rising from their burning village. Saying nothing, their message conveyed with one look, they continued their journey with much sorrow felt in their hearts.

Nearing the end of their long and arduous journey, they reached the coast, a place where they needed to cross. They were stopped by the sight of a huge fire that burnt like a beacon. They assumed from its enormous size there must be a large gathering of people about it, and feared the danger. Legge set out cautiously to investigate. He saw a huge shadow of a figure stood in front of the fire. Legge then heard a voice calling him; as he closed in he saw it was the figure by the fire who called him by his name, it was the Druid he had met on the island. He'd been expecting them, and Legge signalled to Bran that it was safe to approach.

Bran was still only a young boy of eight, but the Druid seemed to be very pleased to meet him. Since the day his father had spoke of him he'd thought of nothing else; he took his hands and looked upon them. Great urgency was now shown to get them to the island. Their arrival had been anticipated and preparations were in order.

There seemed to be no boat present, but they continued to make their crossing on foot. Perhaps, with a low tide, there was some kind of causeway back then that they could walk across?

Legge remained on the mainland; feeling as though he'd kept his father's promise and his commitment was thus fulfilled, he hurriedly returned to his dying father.

Bran was dismayed and angry at his brother's actions and

felt abandoned. He didn't want to be alone; he too wanted to help his father. Led to safety by the Druid, he continually looked back to see his brother riding off back home. He felt so alone. Everyone he'd ever cared for and loved had gone: the mother he had never known; his sister, whom he had failed; his father; and now his brother. Deep in his heart, he knew he'd never see them again. However, he still felt a connection with his sister and believed she was still alive. He hoped that one day he would be strong enough to find her. The Druid tried to put him at his ease until they reached the village where the Druid lived. It was now populated with people of average height, so the Druid stood out amongst the others. Taking time to settle into his new environment, Bran was distant with the strangers.

Under the guidance of the Druid, he came to realise he was special. The Druid taught him of the knowledge he possessed and what was expected of him. Bran continually questioned him; he was particularly interested in the appearance of the sword and its story. Curiosity always left him wanting to know more than he was being told. In return, he was told to be patient. Bran's spare time was spent visiting the twin stones, as he was curiously drawn to them.

Preparations were being made for another large event — a gathering of clans. Bran was sure that this was the event he was being prepared for by the Druid. A sudden influx of people seemed to arrive, more and more each day. Bran was told it was to celebrate the forthcoming solstice and the contest of the sword.

He was awoken early the next day by the Druid; it was the morning of the solstice. It was still dark, but Bran could just make out that the people were making their way to the stones, forming a circle around them. This time there was only one contender in the conquest. Bran recognised him as his father's cousin, the one in charge of the attacking village, the one responsible for the death of his father and brother. Immediately, he was filled with rage. He stood next to the Druid. Frustration continued to grow inside him; it did not go unnoticed by the Druid, who placed a calming hand on his shoulder, controlling his urge to strike out.

The sun began to rise, taking an unusually long time to clear the horizon, the sword appeared. When the sun cleared the horizon, the sword remained. The spectators were filled with excitement as ripples of talk spread amongst them; they knew that the chosen one was present there on the island. With only one contender, the conclusion seemed clear.

Stepping up, the challenger continually looked back smugly at Bran, goading him. He heaved and pulled at the sword with all his strength, but it wouldn't move. He eventually gave up in exhaustion.

Bran seemed confused and looked to the Druid to question him. Looking up, he saw the body of the Druid, but also the familiar face of his father, who spoke: 'My son, you are the chosen one; I urge you to take the sword, and use it well.'

Bran was still only a young boy as he stepped up to the sword, his action not prevented by the onlookers. All the while, he looked back to where he saw his father's face, still looking back at him, urging him to go on. As Bran neared the sword, there was a break in the clouds and a beam of sunlight lit up the sword as he reached out to take it. He was able to remove it from the ground with ease.

The onlookers started closing in on him, chanting his name in elation. Looking out beyond the crowds, his only interest was to see his father's proud face again, yet he was dismayed to only see the Druid as he came forth through the crowds.

Bran asked him, 'Did you see him? Did you see my father?'

The Druid acknowledged him and reassured him that it *was* his father that he saw.

When all was settled, there was a celebration, a feast to celebrate both the solstice and Bran's achievement. During the celebration, his father's cousin approached the Druid and Bran. Bran, wound up with fury, stood before him and raised his sword in readiness to strike.

His father's cousin continued to goad Bran by telling

him how much he had enjoyed killing his father and taking his title. His threats were now directed to Bran, who held that title, a mere boy — it seemed an easy contest. Bran showed no fear and was ready to defend his father's honour, but was stopped by the Druid, who warned, 'The sword has two edges: one to serve you by and one to destroy you by. If you take your own blood, the powers of the sword will cease, thus destroying you.'

Bran now wanted to leave the island. With his new title, he was impatient and felt he had waited long enough. The Druid told him he couldn't leave yet as there was still much to learn. However, Bran owned the sword and its power; he knew he would be protected, and feared nothing; he felt invincible. The Druid had to convince him of the importance of being taught to control the energy and power. With the knowledge and teachings of the Druids came the ability to be at one with nature, to blend into backgrounds, to remain unseen and to be able to control the elements.

Bran was now fifteen years old and much more knowledgeable than he had been before, thanks to the Druid. It felt like a lifetime, living on the island, but in reality it had only been a little more than five years. It was now definitely time that he moved on. With his work complete, the Druid, his mentor, felt it was time for him to move on as well. They both prepared to leave the island and Bran assumed the Druid would be travelling back with him.

On the day of Bran's departure, he and the Druid visited the stones.

Dad felt their reason for doing so was that the stones represented a gateway; they were a place that signified where they had landed on the island and to where they were to leave from.

'This is where my journey ends and yours begins,' the Druid told Bran. 'I must pass to the other world — my time on Earth is at an end. I'm returning to the other world to take my place amongst my ancestors.'

With the mist appearing in readiness, the Druid walked through the ether, bidding farewell to Bran.

Did Bran walk through the same ether? All Dad was aware of was that he crossed the water.

After Bran had crossed the water, he immediately returned home to Gelligaer, where the villagers were expecting him. He was pleased to be met by *Cradog*, his father's closest friend. He'd survived many a battle and was a very brave man. The once present chieftain, Etah's cousin, had been banished. The whole village welcomed Bran home, knowing he was their true leader. Bran was very happy to be home. He made his mark on the cup stone, next to his father's.

The Silures' people were finally reunited under Bran's strength. He regained peace and harmony amongst his people, and with the troubles at an end there was a unity like there'd never been before.

When Bran was not going about his day or hunting, he spent his time with the children in the village; being not that much older than some of them, he told them his stories. He had plenty of time on his hands and was able to relax in these times of peace. Becoming the storyteller, he taught his knowledge and told the tale of his journey, using his magical powers to entertain and bewilder the children.

They were his family now and they regarded him as the 'gentle giant'.

BATTLE AT CAPEL BRITHDIR

12th January 2008.

Dad returned to another familiar place he had regularly visited as a young lad, an old playground haunt. He'd visited Capel Brithdir many times as a child, and something or someone called him there again. Capel Brithdir is the hillside peak of a valley, a steep and tree-lined plateau near his childhood home of Bargoed. Looking back after recent events, Dad and I did wonder if this was where the story truly began. A subliminal clue, 'secrets of the past', lying dormant, waiting to be unlocked — until recently.

Dad was born and raised in Bargoed; he lived with his parents, siblings, grandparents and their children. It was a full but happy household, with often many other additions to their numbers. 'Cappita Brithdir', as he'd known it as a child, was a place often visited as a means of escape and a space to run around in. Dad and his uncle, who were nearly the same age, were often warned by my grandmother to stay well clear. She thought it was too dangerous for them to play there, because of the deep gouges formed on the plateau of the mountain top.

Whilst he played up there one day, near the village of Groes-faen, his uncle fell upon a jagged piece of metal that poked through the ground. It was coppery in colour and covered in Verdigris. Intrigued, they dug it out to find an unusually shaped helmet; a great find for two small boys. They ran home excited and proudly showed off their find. Dad's grandfather was the local rag-and-bone man, and he informed them much to their delight it was an old fireman's helmet. He gave them sixpence for it, its value as scrap metal. This begs the question: what was an old, unusually shaped fireman's helmet doing on the top of a mountain?

It was many years later, as an adult, whilst watching a topical programme on archaeology, the nature of their childhood find was truly revealed. He was amazed by what he saw on the screen before him: an identical helmet to that one found as a boy — a Roman helmet! Not a fireman's helmet after all! Now, that explained why it was found in a place steeped with Roman history.

It confirmed our suspicions that it was another piece of the puzzle, meant to be found by Dad. This story was beginning to twist and turn and connections sprang up that seemed to link together — after all, not all of them could be mere coincidences.

With the sense that this was where the next piece of story would unfold, Dad stood in anticipation. The gouges today are still visible on top of Capel Brithdir, although they have been filled in over the years by farmers, who were losing too many sheep to the perilous pits. The plateau is rock formed and over the centuries, the gouges could be described as movement or land erosion.

The all-too-familiar feeling came to him, with the subtle change to his surroundings and the sense that he wasn't alone. He'd travelled back in time again.

He was now in a time where the Silures, a Celtic tribe who had a stronghold in the area, were moving further inland. They started settling into the valleys and hills that surrounded Gelligaer in order to avoid succumbing to Roman domination. Gelligaer was the site for the Roman settlement and fort, where they sought to defeat and control the Silures. The Romans were hell-bent on taking control of Wales and defeating these proud fighting warriors.

Dad was shown the following events; Bran was calling upon all his chieftains of the outlying villages, to discuss preventing the Romans taking control of their homes. Many meetings had taken place over a lengthy period of time, it seemed. There was a great sense of fear and dread, as after each battle their losses were discussed. Bran was building a picture, learning from his experiences of how the Romans fight, putting much thought into a turnaround of events. He thought of little else other than protecting his people and their future. It was becoming clear to him that fighting on the Romans' terms were impossible. Fighting on flat, open ground with their numbers and weapons gave them a greater strength. If Bran let the Romans set up in their battle formation, they were impenetrable.

Bran was to quickly learn they would only be defeated on his terms, with his knowledge of the land and increasing experience of the Romans and their tactics. Ambush plans were put into action; they used high ground as cover, picking off the Romans in smaller groups and using the element of surprise. These smaller skirmishes were working; the Romans were being defeated whilst marching or setting up camp.

Bran decided that if he couldn't push the Romans back, he'd at least stop them penetrating further inland. Growing in confidence, he continued to use what he'd learnt from his Druid mentor's teachings. Bran's knowledge of the land was his advantage, and the surrounding environment was his best defence. There were several incidents over the next few months where Romans tried to penetrate further inland, yet Bran continually forced them to come over high ground — something the Silures were well adapted too. They ambushed the Romans when they least expected it, picking them off one by one and driving them into bogs, using the land as an ally and defeating them on their own territory.

Although Roman defeat was slow and steady, Bran's eagerness to rid his homeland of the Romans was fierce. He planned his next skirmish, 'a battle to end all battles', and discussed his next moves and plans with his leaders. They were left perplexed by his reasoning, but his warriors put their complete faith in Bran and, as always, trusted his decisions; they knew he had great knowledge of the landscape.

There was still a certain uneasiness as the men climbed

the valley peak (of Capel Brithdir) under the cover of darkness. Setting up camp for the night, there was further talk of battle plans. They lit several large fires on the ridge. These were kept burning throughout the night as beacons, ensuring the Romans are able to see their camp; it seemed Bran was goading them to advance on him.

Before the break of dawn, Bran's men were lined up across the horizon, on top of Capel Brithdir. On either side of them was the steepness of the plateau as it fell away, making the men to feel trapped — what was Bran thinking?

The Romans started their early morning approach via the only way in, outnumbering them by a staggering amount. Bran's men were feeling intimidated by their numbers; they feared great loss and defeat.

Bran had drawn the Romans there deliberately. Capel Brithdir's steep incline presented the Romans with their first challenge: navigating their cavalry to the top. Navigating their siege weapons proved even more difficult and they were therefore left abandoned at the bottom of the hill. The Celts stood anxiously, watching as the Romans struggled to get into their battle formation on uneven ground that they were not accustomed too. Bran's generals were eager strike, to take them by surprise. Still and calm, Bran said nothing, just watched as if in a trance.

Cradog questioned him with a hint of sarcasm, being the only man unafraid to approach Bran, 'How long are you going to wait, until the whole of Rome joins us? Now would be a good time to attack — they're out of formation, unprepared and not ready, exhausted after their climb.'

Bran said nothing.

It was at this point *Cradog* noticed his personality change. The once gentle giant was now possessed with immense hatred against the Romans. His features were distorted with the torment and trouble that had brought him to this. Aggression and defeat were all too clear in his expression, and it was clearly his upmost priority to protect his people.

'I'm not ready to give the order just yet — let them prepare themselves. There is no hurry for victory,' Bran replied. 'The men maybe restless, but they are well rested.

With the Romans complete in their formation, Bran now gave his order, as discussed at their dusk meeting around the campfire. The Celts charged fiercely towards the Romans, who remained steadfast and very aware of their advantage in numbers. Before reaching the Roman frontline, the order was given for them to split into two flanks on the outer edges of the mountain, forming a wide gap. Bran had remained on the spot, his position unchanged, left alone on open ground.

The fear was now felt by the Roman frontline; the stories of 'Bran, the fearsome warrior', with all his powers and magic, had spread. They were mystified by him. What had been an initial raucous of noise was now silent, the air still, the Celts awaited further command.

The Romans, more at ease on the flat ground, felt uneasy now to do battle; they had expected to be ambushed climbing the hill, where they would have been at a disadvantage. The Celts had also wondered why they hadn't made good use of this opportunity.

Bran startled the silence and surprised them all by driving his mighty sword into the ground, twisting it several times. Chanting to himself, with arms raised to the sky, dark thunderous clouds appeared over the plateau. Lightening filled the sky, terrifying the Romans; one huge bolt struck Bran's sword several times, causing the ground to shudder. Before him the ground opened up into huge cracks. Running directly from Bran across the hilltop in several directions were cracks several metres wide and several metres deep, heading in the direction of the Romans. The Celts in their outer flank position stood well clear of the appearing cracks. It was a fearsome sight Dad saw before him, as Romans and horses began to fall into the deep crevices. Those standing behind were dragged in; some men trying to help became victims themselves as they fell in. It was utter carnage, with many bodies clambering to save themselves.

The Celts, still in their split formation, continued down the mountainside to surround the remaining Romans. Chased down the hillside of Groes-faen, Romans were picked off one by one as they scrambled to their death. Bran, still in his original position, looked down at the huge gorges. With the deed done, he stamped his foot on the ground and the cracks began to close up, swallowing all that had fallen in.

Dad was left shaken at the unbelievable sight of the mountain closing in on everything, seeing men and horses crushed as they disappeared. The gruesome noise of dying men and beasts filled his head, cries of distress, men screaming out in fear and agony. He'd put his hands to his ears to diffuse the awful, blood-curdling noise. Dad then realised the noise was not a physical one but an internal noise in his head.

Dad could not understand how these events were possible. The power and magic Bran possessed were unbelievable! However, the scars on the hilltop today were clearly visible. Could this be a possible reason to their existence? Bran was indeed a very powerful and awesome Druid. The crevices are clearly visible on the mountain today, although they have slowly been filled in over the years by farmers wanting to protect their livestock from falling. These crevices also happen to be situated near the area where Dad unearthed the Roman helmet.

Bran was left alone in the aftermath; he stood silent with his face buried in his hands. When he took them from his face, he found his hands were dripping with blood — a symbol of the bloodshed he'd caused. He washed them in a nearby stream, trying hard to rid them of the blood, then spent the night alone on top of the mountain in deep contemplation, thinking about the misery and agony that was caused by his deeds. He was a broken man and didn't understand why it had to be like this. Once a gentle giant, loving and caring as a child, he hated the monster he'd become.

Sometime after the battle, his friend *Cradog* returned to the hilltop seeking Bran. He noticed that he was different from the Bran he'd seen earlier at the battle. He now seemed like the young Bran he'd once known — youthful almost — shedding tears of pain and suffering. Gone was the madness he'd witnessed at the start of battle.

Bran said, 'All will be well.' He then dismissed him, as he wanted to be left alone with his thoughts. In his solitude, he remembered the family he had lost and thought fondly of his father, Etah.

Throughout the portrayals of Bran's nature, he seemed to have a split personality. His true nature is one of goodness, gentleness and kindness, mainly because of his upbringing and family. He was a typical Celt, an almighty leader with a sense of community. His Druid training helped him to bring peace and tranquillity to his people and brought with it a love of nature... but evil lurked beneath. It was an evil that lay deep within him, a monster that reared its ugly head and caused bloodshed. A battle was going on inside his mind, and he became tormented, teetering between a real hatred of the Romans and a need to do what was best for his people. Bran ignored his good nature and convinced himself he was evil and destructive; he blamed himself for the massacre. Killing was not in his nature, and therefore the guilt and shame of killing fellow humans, even if they were Roman, led him to some sort of mental breakdown.

The battle at Capel Brithdir was over — or so Bran thought. True enough, the Romans had been defeated. He was unable to completely wash the blood from his hands and he still struggled with his conscience. The blood appeared to remind him of what he'd done; he tried continuously to rid himself of it, to no avail. The stream flowed red, emulating the colour of blood, but his hands remained stained. Bran was left feeling angry with himself, tortured by the death that had followed him in his own life with the loss of his loved ones and for the death he had caused to others. He convinced himself that he had done what he had to when it came to the Romans; it wasn't done out of malice or hatred. It was necessary, for the sake of his people and their future. He had fought for what was right.

BRAN AND *CRADOG'S* DAUGHTER

54 AD.

Bran's solitude on Capel Brithdir was disturbed before dawn by his general, *Cradog*. Like his father, *Cradog* was a fine man and they had been good friends for many years, fighting alongside one another in battle. Now *Cradog* served under Bran's leadership, and felt privileged to do so. As he approached, Bran noticed his appearance; there were scars on his face — the marks of a tremendous battle.

A further battle had taken place between some Romans who had been waiting in the village for the returning Celts from the battle at Capel Brithdir. *Cradog* had been captured and tortured, and was beaten into submission to send word to Bran. The Romans were giving an ultimatum: either Bran surrendered himself, or the hostages, the captured villagers, would be slaughtered. It seemed the civilised Romans were indeed the barbaric ones, not the Celts, who fought in an attempt at self-preservation and defence.

Cradog stepped up to Bran, explaining while simultaneously struggling with his thoughts. Another part of the Roman army had invaded the village. They were ambushed on their return and many of his men had been killed with the village, its women, children and elders, taken as hostages. Those that had not been captured had fled into the hills.

'I have been sent to find you against my will, to send you word,' *Cradog* told Bran.

Bran asked about *Arianwyn*.

'Yes, she too has been taken,' said *Cradog*. 'Bran, the Romans want an exchange: your life for the lives of your people.'

Bran's feelings for *Arianwyn, Cradog's* daughter, had blossomed from friendship into love. They have grown up together, and she had been a close friend of his sister. She was there the day Hadean was taken, and understood his pain. She loved him dearly in return and she always saw the good in him.

How he wished things could have been different! Yet again another loved one so tragically taken from him. In his short life he had suffered so much tragedy, losing those around him whom he loved so dearly. The day he lost his sister was always on his mind, her memory haunting him, sharing a strange connection as twins do... He still saw her in his dreams. He felt her pain and her happiness, but even with all the powers he possessed, still he was unable to find her. It took its toll on his mind. He was at breaking point mentally as he heard the news of *Arianwyn* and his people. He wanted no further executions; he didn't want to be responsible for any more bloodshed — especially his beloved *Arianwyn* and his people.

Cradog pleaded with Bran not to give in to the demands of the Romans. He was not only a great leader and warrior but an inspiration to his men — what would they do without his command?! However, Bran didn't fear the Romans and was willing to return with *Cradog* and agree to their terms. He would do this for his people, as he knew only too well that if the women and children were killed there would be no future generations. He could not see that happen, for then he truly would be defeated. He may appear ruthless, but he was far from it. He had two sides torn between love and ruthlessness: the one that destroys only where necessary for the sake of his people (like the sword he carried that possessed light and dark forces), and the loving, caring, remorseful side. His Druidic training had nurtured him to be peace-loving; he was not the barbaric monster the Romans were led to believe. He only did his best, as any leader would, to protect his people and was filled with remorse at killing human beings.

Cradog returned to face the Romans, regretfully leading

Bran to the stone circle. Bran was ready to release his conscience and in return set free his people and his beloved *Arianwyn.*

He told *Cradog,* 'Take the people to the high ground, where the men under your command will keep them safe. Send my love to your daughter, *Arianwyn.* Then return and meet me back here at sunrise on the second day — bring with you my horse and my sword.' He left the sword and horse with *Cradog* with a reminder to return at second sunrise.

Bran gave himself freely to the Romans and was prepared for what they would do to him. At first they shackled his feet and hands; the Romans feared him, even chained up they are nervous of him. They were scared to just be near him. He was huge and menacing to them. All Bran wanted was freedom for his people, and he was prepared to sacrifice himself to get it — or at least, he was prepared to let the Romans think that. When they knew he was secure, they released his people. Bran had been given word that his people were free. His thoughts were for *Arianwyn;* the love he felt inside gave him strength and control for what lay ahead.

The Romans held a trial for him, and he was tried with crimes against Rome and its Emperor. Even though the Romans knew the outcome, they liked to do things by the book, going through the motions. Bran was sentenced to death by crucifixion.

As Bran was sat silently in his holding cell, he heard them making his cross, as the crucifixion was to take place at sunrise. The cross was unlike the one you would imagine; this one was shaped like the letter T. Bran was calm and untroubled by what lay ahead; it was the past that troubled him.

At sunrise Bran was taken outside. There before him, flat on the ground, lay his cross. There was no force used by the Romans; he positioned himself on the cross peacefully whilst soldiers tied his arms and legs into position. Another soldier appeared, trembling uncontrollably; carrying extremely large nails of a strange shape. Halfway down the nail there were square pegs that jutted out. The jutted-out peg rested on his flesh when hammered into place. They began with his feet, and then worked upwards — not to his hands, but his wrists. They wanted him dead, and quickly.

Bran didn't flinch or move a muscle, nor did he make a sound. There was no expression on his face. Once again, it was like he'd put himself under a spell, hypnotised into a trance. He felt no pain, and all the while he remembered the face and love of *Arianwyn*. Strangely, there was no blood either. The soldiers were bemused; they couldn't understand it, he should have been in tremendous pain and bleeding. Ropes were tied to the cross for hoisting it into the ground, and there several soldiers were needed to take this immense weight. The thud of the cross as it hit the bottom of the hole caused the earth to shudder. All the while Bran's head was on his chest. Finally, he was upright, and he then raised his head. His eyes glowed with blue beams of light. Within minutes it had gone from sunrise to a midday sun shining above them. The picture was being sped up; the clouds raced across the sky, the slowly rising sun was up and over Bran's head, quickly moving towards its setting position.

The sun stopped behind the cross, casting a huge shadow on the ground. Everything in that shadow burst into flames, consuming people and burning the ground beneath them. There was panic and fear, and every Roman was trying to escape the shadow. It remained like that for hours, until time had caught up with the advancing sun, and it was able to set naturally in its own time.

When darkness fell, even though the night sky was clear, the moon was nowhere to be seen. There was not a star in the sky, just complete blackness. The Romans feared that the Celts would come and remove their leader under the cover of darkness, so they posted sentries at four corners to prevent this. Two stood at the rear, with several guarding the perimeter around the front. At sunrise, the guards were being prepared for relief of night sentries. As they approached they noticed there was something strange afoot, and an odd feeling came over them when they saw no men on duty. There was no trace of them, not even a dropped weapon — nothing. The new sentries were approaching from the back of the cross and they were very afraid, especially when they saw two pools of fresh blood on the ground, under the outstretched arms of the cross.

They hesitated to look, even though they knew for sure Bran was dead, because any normal being would have bled to death. One soldier was brave enough venture to the front, fear pounding in his chest. Bran was no longer on the cross. Instead, there upon the cross were the two rear sentries, tied and nailed on top of each other. It was their blood on the ground. When they were cut down, the expressions on their faces were contorted with fear; they had literally been scared to death before being crucified.

* * *

Bran feared the darkness each time it consumed him; his spirit was being dissolved and he found it more and more difficult to return to normality.

As promised, *Cradog* was once again amazed to see Bran alive. He met Bran at the stone circle with his horse and sword, unaware of the events that had taken place. Bran, on the other hand, was delusional with anger and in a very confused state of mind. He told *Cradog* he had to leave, and soon, for everyone's safety. Bran was angry with himself and no longer wanted this power. He then said his goodbyes and made his retreat.

Heading down through the valley, he then disappeared to the boggy ground of the marshland, to make his offering to the gods. He threw the sword into the boggy water, offering it to Seulus, the god of water, as a sacrifice. In exchange he wanted to be cleansed, to rid himself of the blood from his hands and the overpowering darkness. He reached into the water to wash his hands; feeling a strange connection he raised his hands from the water to find he was holding his sword. Bran was even more confused, and needed to get away urgently. If he stayed, death and destruction would surely follow him.

Bran hoped he could return the sword as an offering back to where it belonged; he just wanted to be cleansed.

There was much confusion as to why the sword was unable to be returned to the water. The god of water, did not want it, and so he had refused to take the offering. Therefore, Bran's only option was to return it to Anglesey where it came from. However, his need for the sword was not over yet.

ARIANWYN

54 AD.

Meanwhile, the Romans constantly searched for the whereabouts of Bran. First stop was his village at Gelligaer. There was no one there, but they burnt it to the ground anyway.

Winter was on its way, and the Romans were leaving Gelligaer to head off to their winter quarters.

When safe to do so, the village saw the return of its people, who had remained in hiding since Bran left. They immediately began rebuilding their homes before winter could set in.

Arianwyn carried Bran's child, and feared for the unborn child's safety and that of her own. She told no one of her condition — not even her parents. She feared they would be angry with her — as angry as they were with Bran for leaving. However, she feared the Romans more, knowing too well what they'd be capable of! If they knew she was carrying Bran's child, she would also be hunted down. The winter months and the added layers of clothing hid the pregnancy well. It soon became harder to disguise her changing body and it was not too long before her mother noticed. She shared her fears with her mother, but still they said nothing to *Cradog*.

When spring arrived, *Arianwyn* decided to leave the village alone. She intended to go to a neighbouring village to stay with relations there. Telling no one, not even her mother, she left.

When her father found out she'd gone, his wife told

him of her condition. He had an idea where she might be heading. He set out on horseback immediately, travelling all day to get to where he was going, only to be disappointed to find she was not there. Exhausted, he stayed the night, and planned to leave the following morning.

Arianwyn didn't complete her journey; when only half way, she was struck down by the pains of labour and gave birth to a baby daughter. She rested, exhausted...

The following morning, on his return journey, *Cradog* paused, thinking he'd heard a baby crying. His mind was playing tricks, surely. Continuing, he heard it again, following the sounds this time. When he found *Arianwyn* his heart sank; she was weak, surrounded by so much blood, barely alive as she held her baby.

She was so happy and relieved to see the familiar face of her father. *Cradog* cradled them both in his arms, comforting them in a rocking motion, until she slipped away.

Cradog sat motionless, holding the child. He couldn't leave his daughter there in the open, where the wild animals could reach her. He gently prepared her body for her cremation, as was their way.

He then returned to the village; the baby needed feeding, and there were new mothers in the village that would be able to help. He explained his daughter was staying with relations and, on his return, he found the abandoned baby. This way no one knew of the mother or father, even though the child bore the birthmark of Bran's family.

Cradog and his wife adopted the child as their own.

He returned to *Arianwyn* to collect her ashes, placing them into an urn before burying her properly in the ground with offerings of personal items, beads and food.

RETURN TO ANGLESEY

Spring 2008.

With the visions Dad had been shown and the knowledge that these twin stones at Anglesey were still in existence, it became all too clear that he must pay them a visit. The timing of the next event coincided with the beginning of the summer solstice, a very important time in the Druid calendar. It had to be now, otherwise he got the feeling that he'd have to wait until the following year. One thing that he'd realised was that there was no forcing the events to happen; they occurred by themselves, in their own time.

Living in South Wales, with Anglesey being as far into North Wales as you can possibly get, Dad set out in the early hours of the morning to get there in good time and avoid the traffic. With no map or guidelines and having never been that far north in Wales before, he set out with just his instincts and the feeling he would be shown the way. Driving through the darkness to be there at sunrise seemed important.

It was almost dawn when Dad reached the stones successfully, after over four hours of driving non-stop to reach his destination. From where he parked the car at a nearby farm, he could see the dark shadows of the stones looming at Penrhos Feilw. Feeling once again cautious, he began his approach through the farm gate into the field where they stood. The sun began to rise, reflecting on the stones and picking up the white shards of stone against the greyness that lay within. As the sun glistened upon them they twinkled like stars; mesmerised, Dad hadn't realised the slight change of his surroundings. The stones looked different, upright and somewhat larger... As he looked round, he found he could not see the farm anymore and he realised he was inside another vision.

Dad continued to walk towards the stones, getting closer. Between the stones appeared a silvery blue, ethereal mist, but the stones remained clear as the sun rose around them. Behind the mist was a brightness, but it did not come from the sun, as the sun was behind him.

Now the pull began; he was being drawn towards the mist... He stopped briefly, and alongside him appeared Bran, who was making the same journey through the mist. This must be the next event — was this where Bran had retreated after leaving Gelligaer and *Arianwyn*? Dad's heart beat faster as Bran passed by — he was so close that his face could be seen clearly.

Bran's head bowed as if in shame and he looked down upon his hands. The blood was still dripping from them and clearly caused him pain and sorrow. He felt great remorse for the pain he'd caused. He was still a young man, and had not changed much since Dad last saw him at Capel Brithdir; he had shoulder-length hair, and was clean-shaven with a boyish face. However, it was much contorted, muddled and sad. Dad sensed the two sides of him, like a split personality: the good side — kind, remorseful and filled with sorrow — and the other side — strong, determined and remorseless for what he'd done. This latter side felt he had done what was necessary, what any great leader would have done, in defending his territory and protecting his people. The Romans were set upon invading his territory, causing death and destruction for anyone who got in their way.

There was a sense that Bran was returning to the underworld to cleanse his spirit, to rid him of this confusion. It seemed he wanted to be the person he had been before he'd become this monster with destruction in his heart. Killing was not in his nature — it had only become part of him through circumstance. As Bran passed by, he was not aware of Dad and disappeared through the mist.

The mist drew Dad towards it. He felt a little less anxious, yet he was not afraid; he was used to these situations by now. On the other side of the mist the stones were no longer there; they seemed to be some gateway or portal. Whilst standing before the stones at Anglesey the sea had been before him, but now the sea was behind him. Spiritually, he'd been transported to another place and time and no longer felt like he was in Anglesey, but in Ireland.

The era was much further back in time, well before Bran — almost 2,000 years before. He was in the northern part of Ireland, near the coast, and close by there was a large expanse of water. Having had previous visions of this area Dad recognised the land. Living around this area of water were many people, a close-knit community, with surrounding villages and extended families. There was one ruler for them all. They all looked alike, being around seven-feet tall, fair-haired and fair-skinned. They all had blue eyes and similar facial features.

Apart from this race, which appeared to be that of a Druid community, there were others on the island. These further villages were of a different race, more Celtic in nature and appearance. Their height varied but the majority were of average height, standing at around five feet tall, and they all looked very different from one another. Through a natural process of migration, they had integrated with other villages of their kind. Their community had expanded greatly and they were closing in around the Druid community.

There was a sense that this Celtic race carried some kind of disease or plague; there were many sick individuals within their community. Despite this, it seemed their immune system was far stronger than that of the Druid people, who seemed to have a smaller gene pool. Migration had moved them so close together that disease has entered one of the Druid villages, and within no time it had spread from village to village, wiping out almost the entire Druid community. All that remained was the village of their ruler and his extended family.

They had good reason to believe why they escaped the

fatal disease. In their possession they had a 'sacred stone' that had fallen from the gods to protect them. The stone was gold and silver in appearance.

The legend of the stone is one that has been passed down from generation to generation.

In the beginning, the Druids believed there was no darkness; only daylight existed. This being because they had two suns or, as they believed, two fathers, who provided their source of heat for food and for life. As one sun rested the other rose to take its place. This was a gift from the gods that gave them the light and sustenance, so their vegetation grew rapidly and well. However, in time, the land became hot under these conditions. Day never ended and there was no rest for the earth that they believed was their mother, the place where they returned after death. Seas began to shrink and rivers became dry. The people of that time became unhappy, praying to the gods for only one 'father', or sun. Being mostly fishermen, they wanted to restore their rivers and seas that were their source of food supply. They longed not only for one mother, but one father. Therefore, they prayed. It was not long before their prayers were answered. The two suns met in the sky together as everyone watched, getting closer and closer as they prepared for battle. Clashing together, they battled to be sole ruler of the skies. Eventually, one sun lost its battle, losing all its power and light, and emerged as a white shadow of a former sun. The former sun fell to the ground, like golden stardust trailing it's lost soul. The gold they later found in the ground, they believed to be that of the former sun. A larger piece was found, the 'sacred stone', and was believed to be the ex-sun's soul. It was taken to the King. Being a gift from the gods, it was believed to be sacred and bring them protection.

This was why they felt they'd been spared from disease: the stone was still in their possession when the fatal disease hit their people. However, as the majority of their population was wiped out from the disease, there was much concern. Each year that followed more people died than were being born. Many of those who *were* born did not survive; it was about one in four that did survive. Those that did survive were predominately female. There was great fear amongst the dwindling Druid community and they kept within their boundaries, maintaining their distance from the migrating race. Each year the population grew smaller and they believed even though they were protected by their 'sacred stone' they were in grave danger of becoming extinct. The King's wife had given birth to several children, none of which survived. The King, fearful there would be no heir, thus decided to take a younger wife in the hope that new blood would provide an heir. Time, they felt, was against them and they no longer felt safe there. They no longer believed that the land was going to provide them with a secure future, so they had to move on. Once again the King and shaman asked the gods to show them the way.

Whilst the men were on their usual fishing trip, they came across one of the Celts washed up on the beach. He was barely alive when they decided to help him. They retrieved his nearby boat and took the contents and the man back to their village. Initially they feared him, because of the disease, but were convinced the 'sacred stone' would protect them. They saw him as having been sent by the gods. In his boat they found a sack of what looked like tools, and so they assumed he was a trader. They seemed to be of a similar colour to that of their 'sacred stone', which convinced them even more he'd been sent from the gods. It was certainly something they'd never seen before; they still used flint and rock. A few days passed and, being well looked after, the trader made a full recovery and befriended his carers, giving them his tools as a gift. He described how he used them for work and not weapons.

On a clear day he took the King for a stroll to the water's edge. Pointing across the water, he saw the land from whence he came. He told the King if the weather was just right it was an easy crossing, one that he'd made several times himself. During his last crossing, the weather had not been good; the sea had been rough, causing him to part company with his boat and become swept up onto the beach. The King wanted to know more of the crossing and told the trader of his eagerness to leave this troubled land. With his help they began immediately to build bigger boats. They were able to build the boats quicker with the use of their new tools and the knowledge passed on by their new friend.

During this time the King's new wife became pregnant, by the time the boats were built, the baby was almost due. The weather was not ideal to travel straight away and the King was advised to wait for more suitable conditions. But with the child due to be born any day now, the King feared if they stayed any longer and the child was born it wouldn't survive. Eager to leave, the King ignored the good advice, taking the risk for a better chance of survival. Therefore, it was by the King's word that they left. The sea was dotted with lots of boats — at least a hundred. Their journey began well but soon they were engulfed and held back by a sweeping fog. He was advised to tie as many boats together as possible, so when it lifted they would at least remain together. Fearing the fog, they frantically began tying their boats together, wanting to arrive safely together. The fog lasted all of that day and well into the night, and when it lifted the skies were overcast, with no sign of the moon and not a star in the sky. They looked in every direction but couldn't see land. They drifted all day without a clue as to where they were. As dusk fell, they spied land ahead and were determined to reach it before darkness fell; they feared that nightfall would hamper their journey, causing them to lose sight of land again.

Arriving on shore, they moved inland to the high ground. It was unfamiliar territory for their friend the Celt; it seemed they had drifted way off course, landing at Anglesey. The next few nights were spent lighting fires on the high ground as beacons to those boats that had broken their bonds and remained lost. Days passed and it was only those boats that had remained tied together that made it to the same shore; a quarter remained lost or had landed elsewhere.

The King's wife went into labour during the night and a son was born; because he was born at night the people believed it was a bad omen. This stemmed from the legend of the two suns. The King was relieved and pleased the child was alive and a male heir. However, he was surprised to see his wife was still in labour at dawn; another son was born at a good time and was considered an even bigger blessing to the King. Feeling doubly blessed, to celebrate and commemorate their births and to give thanks to the gods for their safe journey and his sons, the twin stones were erected. The stones were cut from the rock face and shaped, the rock chosen particularly because of the sparkly white flecks. Moving his people had been the right thing to do and he believed the gods were happy. He also believed that as long as the stones stood tall and strong, then so would his sons.

The stones were not just symbolic to the birth of the twins but they also stood as guardians to the gateway, from this world to the underworld; to them a place of peace and re-birth. Their new friend they'd found on the beach stayed with the Druid community. One day the King showed him their 'sacred stone' that protected them. With his knowledge, the Druid recognised it as metal ore and convinced the King he could change the stone into a sword, a weapon so powerful it would be feared by many, making him an almighty King. With great faith in his new friend the King granted him permission to go ahead.

After many days of removing the ore, smelting and shaping it, the sword was complete. It was indeed a sight to behold, the colours shone brightly. As the King was of great stature, the sword was uniquely created for him and so was also huge in size. What he'd created was truly a unique sword — the inner blade golden in colour like the sun, the cutting edges silvery blue like the moon. These different metals appeared to give the added strength and beauty, and its power would protect against all its enemies.

As the twins were growing up, the King knew there could only be one heir. The older twin frequently asked whom he'd name as his heir. The King knew he couldn't choose between them; they were both precious gifts and each had special qualities.

The King called upon the shaman, the elder of the

village, for his knowledge and communication with the gods. The boys were indeed very different: one kind and gentle the other strong and fearless. Both would make a good king. The shaman and the King headed off to the twin stones to seek advice from the gods. As they approached the stones, they looked up into the sky and saw the unusual sight of the sun and moon close together. They were both concerned and knew of the legend of the two suns and their battle. What they feared now was that the shadow of the lost sun sought revenge. Before their eyes, they saw the moon swallow the sun, and darkness spread across the land. They were terrified that the darkness would remain and the sun lost forever. They took this to symbolise that the elder son would destroy the younger to become heir. Taking his newly made sword, the King thrust it into the darkness as an offering to the gods, hoping that they would take what once fell from the sky back.

There was a beam of light as the moon left the sun, and the first ray of light appeared on the land, directly between the two stones, and there in the ground was the sword standing upright in the light. This was the sign they'd waited for, and the King tried to remove his sword from the ground but couldn't.

The shaman, as if in a trance, spoke not with his own voice but with an unfamiliar one: 'This is the test the gods have set for your sons: the one who is worthy of being king will be able to remove the sword from the ground.'

He returned from his trance, unaware of the words he'd spoken. The shaman was to become the guardian of the sword. Dad came out of that vision and into the here and now; he was returned through the stones and the mist to the other side where he'd started; he was back on Anglesey.

Following close behind, he saw Bran appear from the mist, his face now free from pain and anguish. There was no blood on his hands and he appeared to be a different person, cleansed and content. Dad followed him to what he saw as a large Celtic settlement, or rather, the remains of what was once the large village before it was burnt to the ground. Bran picked up a handful of ashes; there was no bones in there and so he assumed the villagers had fled in time. Venturing further afield, he found the surrounding villages were also burnt to the ground. Wandering aimlessly, he came across a young man tending to some goats. The young man was frightened by Bran's size — he'd never seen anyone that huge before. Bran convinced the young man he meant him no harm and asked where the villagers have gone.

The young man replied, 'They're all dead.'

Bran was confused and said, 'But.... I was only here yesterday.'

'Not so, it can't be, I was a child when the villages were destroyed by the Romans,' was the young man's reply.

So, what had been many years away had only felt like yesterday to Bran, and the Romans had reached and destroyed these villages in Anglesey, far north of his home in Gelligaer. He was filled with rage at the mere mention of the Romans and felt angeredby what they had done.

Surely not all were killed, he thought, maybe some had been taken as prisoners or slaves. One thing he was sure about, there had been much bloodshed and he had to return home to Gelligaer. His main thoughts were of *Arianwyn* and her fate; he was angry with himself for leaving her when he should have been there to protect her and his people. Anger consumed him once again at the mere thought of the Romans' destruction. Dad then saw a huge bird, like an eagle, perched on the branch of a nearby tree. He sensed that somehow Bran took this form to return home, and with the same urgency, Dad also wanted to return home. However, he was going to stay overnight and drive back the following day, after some more sightseeing. He took some photos of the stones before he left, still feeling their warmth, as if they had heartbeats. When he looked upon the one stone, he had a strange feeling and sensed it was almost like a mummified body, with the sinews and flesh of a corpse.

On his way home, all he could think of was how the twin had carried the stone all that way from Anglesey over mountains and rough terrain to Gelligaer.

The Twin Stones of Penrhos Feilw, Anglesey.

REUNITED AT LAST

Summer 2008.

Up until now, Calla had remained Dad's guardian angel, being in constant connection with him. Now she seemed to be conveying feelings that the story and events that have happened were ending.

After Dad's return from Anglesey, he felt no urgency to return to the cemetery. It wasn't untill the following day that the feelings became present, at around the usual time of early evening, when the sun was low in the sky. This had been a significant factor throughout previous events. Dad had expected the same guidance to the cemetery, but this did not happen. This time, Dad was totally in control of this visit. Only part of him hoped this to be the final journey and time for Calla to part company with him.

This time he decided to take the more direct route, along the higher road, to the place where he had found the coin. His surroundings were familiar and of the present day when he entered the cemetery. On approaching the initial place where it all began, his surroundings slowly changed to those of the past.

Close to him was the vision of five children playing by a brook. They were throwing stones in the water and having great fun. The children were small, except for the boy who approached them from a distance; he was much bigger in size. Dad wondered what the significance of these children was in the story.

Suddenly, a man on a galloping white steed approached, forcing the children to scatter and hide in fear. The taller boy was still advancing, seeing the children scatter — all but his sister, who was too young to be aware of the danger. As she stood by the brook, she was swept up into the arms of the rider.

The young boy, trying to protect his sister, ran into the pathway of the oncoming steed to stop it. The horse reared, knocking him to the ground as the captor rode off.

Picking himself up off the ground, unafraid, the boy furiously threw stones at the rider, pursuing the horse in frustration. Dad saw the face of the young girl clearly, and was slightly confused to recognise it as the face of the slave girl he'd seen at Herculaneum.

The girl called out to the boy in distress, 'Bran...Bran!'

The boy replied, 'Hady... Hady!'

The vision disappeared and, as Dad continued to walk on, there was a sudden blinding bright light, causing Dad to close his eyes. On opening them, he was now faced with the boy from his vision. It was clearly Bran. Even as a child, his stature was manlike, and he blocked out the sun that lay huge in the background. He stood steadfastly, wishing Dad to go no further.

Both of them heard a child's voice; she called out, 'Bran? Bran?'

Bran recognised the voice.

Where Bran had stood alone, Dad now saw the two children: Bran, and the child he only knew as Calla. Another piece was added to the puzzle. They were holding hands, their beaming faces plainly showing they were pleased to finally be reunited.

So this had been the reason why Calla wanted to return so much! Gelligaer had once been her true home and she was now reunited with her twin brother! Hadean was home. This vision also disappeared and Dad continued onwards, towards the direction of the sun.

Before him appeared four figures, three adults and a child. They appeared as physical entities, their faces clear and unmistakeable. All four were smiling and happy — even Bran had an expression of contentment, a real difference to the persona Dad had seen of him so far!

There was a strange closeness between them all and a sense of forgiveness. With a sense of relief and spiritual contentment, Dad felt he had completed his journey, and the task asked of him by Cateus that seemed to have been said an age ago.

Cateus was the voice heard out of the silence: 'The journey, although not over, is only short from here; you are our ferryman and you have to go with us and guide us through to the other side.'

Anxiety gripped Dad once again, and he was filled with fear of the unknown. What was it he was asking? It was this part of the journey he'd feared more than all the rest, but it felt too late not to see it through to the end.

In the background appeared a tunnel of light, surrounded by what seemed like a dark place. Knowing it was his job to lead the way, the fear of being the first to enter was overwhelming. Dad screwed up his courage and put his complete trust in the spirits, who had become familiar companions; he hoped they would continue to protect him.

Through the light, they travelled downwards, spiralling to reach the other side. Coming to a halt, they were now stood at the bank of a river. The water flowed swiftly as the spirits stepped into the water to make their crossing. They walked along the surface and expected Dad to follow — how would it be possible for him to do the same as them? Dad couldn't swim and he feared the current would take him. Ignoring the fear in the pit of his stomach, he walked across with them and safely reached the other side.

On the other side, it was a remarkable sight; as bright and warm as a summer's day, with the scent of woodland trees. Lush green grass and fragrant flowers filled the air; it was a scene bursting with life and colour. There was a serene sense of peace and tranquillity. Dad couldn't help feel it would be the kind of place anyone would be happy to stay for the rest of their days. However, Dad knew he had to make the journey back alone.

Standing with them in the lush surroundings, their physical presence became more solid and clear. Contentment on their faces, they faced Dad and bowed their heads in appreciation for what he had done.

Cateus spoke softly. 'I cannot thank you enough for what you've done; it was everything I asked of you and more. For that I will be eternally grateful.

'Now you must return home and to your family. We'll never forget you, as much as you won't forget us. Although you have to return alone, you'll know the way. No matter what you see or hear, don't look back — trust in what I say.'

As he began his short journey back, there was a strange sense with him, another presence, and he heard a familiar voice. It was the voice of his mother, also present in the afterlife. He was sorely tempted to look around and see his mother standing there, but he remembered what Cateus had told him and believed it was a trick on his mind, an aim to make him lose his way.

Not straying from his path, he was eager to be with his family again — although he was upset that he had ignored his mother's voice. His need to see her once again had been so strong.

When he returned to his own time, it was almost dusk and he was filled with overwhelming, mixed emotions. Happiness was his strongest feeling, having fulfilled his tasks and completed his amazing journey. He'd seen Cateus and Hygieia in the presence of Calla once again, and Calla's identity had been explained as the long lost sister of Bran. Hadean had been reunited with her twin and her homeland.

All the pieces of the puzzle were now neatly slotted into place, especially the confusion about Hygieia's birthmark and where she had inherited it. Dad now knew it was from Bran's side of the family, hence Calla also had it.

Dad sat for a moment, looking back at his epic journey, putting all the pieces into perspective so that it all became even clearer in his mind.

He was grateful for the protection and guidance he had gotten from spirits he had met along the way; he felt as content as Cateus felt. Filled with relief, he returned home.

Like Bran, Dad has now passed to the other side, to the afterlife. Like a true Druid, his journey was filled with magic and tales only legends are made of. This books tells his tale — a story to pass onto his ancestors, marking a huge turning point in his life.

CONCLUSION

It still amazes me today that Dad experienced all these amazing journeys, passing through time and meeting these extraordinary characters. It gave me insight and a deeper fascination into the supernatural, and it encouraged me to conduct further research into Druidic life and Celtic culture.

I have been both intrigued and moved by Bran's life, and the tragic choices he made in difficult circumstances. I found it interesting to discover how interpretations through history can be so biased and full of propaganda. The Celts merely defended their lands against their Roman invaders and protected their people as best as they could. It was the power-hungry Romans who came to conquer lands by slaughtering everyone who stood in their way.

As I began my journey to record these events, the facts and coincidences along the way became all too obvious. Each event my findings linked to left me another clue to research, and when I found what I was looking for I was even more intrigued and so wanted to prove their validity.

My first task led me to validate the coin. We knew it dated from much earlier than when the Romans occupied Gelligaer, and there was evidence that it had been in a fire. This would certainly tie up with story told by its previous owner. However, I wanted to know more, so I had the coin examined by a medium through psychometry.

She was able to tell me that the coin didn't belong to me. Apparently, the previous owner had suffered great anguish and torment, and had met with a violent, untimely end. This certainly summed up Cateus' life!

The birthmark possessed by Hygieia and Calla was another coincidence. It turned out it was the family birthmark of Violet and Morita — that's two recent generations on my paternal side — and Dad's uncle still had this mark. This research led to further discoveries. My grandfather had sickle cell anaemia. For those of you aware of this disorder, it can really only be found in Afro-Caribbean or Mediterranean provenances. My grandfather was white and, after researching my family history as far back to the mid-1800s, I have found no evidence of either Afro-Caribbean or Mediterranean lineage. I only found that my grandfather mentioned ancestors of Romany gypsy provenance. Other than that, my great-grandmother Violet did have some kind of blood disorder which I believe resulted from a B12 deficiency. For this she received regular injections, as my dad recalls, and seemed quite obvious now that she must have been a carrier of the sickle cell. Both parents can carry it, but the female is most often the carrier, passing it onto a male offspring. So, it could be quite possible this came from Romany/Mediterranean ancestors.

Another coincidence occurs in the dreams, with Dad waking up continually at 4am. This is quite possibly the time Calla died all those years ago. However, those that appeared in the dream were Cateus and Hygieia and both of them died during times of darkness, around 4pm — as had Bran!

Dad went missing on the day of his first supernatural occurrence around 6:30pm and returned home around 9pm. The place where he'd been taken to was the very spot where he'd found the coin back in 1993 — the very year Dad had become a grandfather for the first time. The coin itself was a mystery, as it's dated around 33 – 43 AD. Quite plausibly, the reason lies within the story: the coin had once belonged to Calla, in a time where she would have been a young woman in Rome. The fact is the Romans didn't arrive in Wales until around 60 AD, over twenty years after the coin was minted. More coincidental was that the cremation in the vision had taken place where the coin was found — evidence that the coin had been in a fire!

In recorded history, Servius Galba had a wife and two sons, which he tragically lost. However, he never remarried, despite the fact he was pursued by the beautiful Agrippa, Nero's mother. One thing that can also be said of the Romans, especially those of a more superior stature: they had many an affair. In most instances, these affairs often involved their own slaves, who almost considered it their duty to take part. Again, this signals it may be true that Calla carried an Emperor's child and possibly points to, as the story tells, another reason why Cateus, a mere slave, was given such opportunities and freedom.

Research after the events also produced evidence that there was a house at Herculaneum that had belonged to Galba. Another coincidence or evidence of plausibility? Galba's house was the last section of the site at Herculaneum to be excavated — and this occurred at the time when Dad was having the dreams! Could this have unearthed the psychic connection?

Other strange clues led us to find that Epidaurus did indeed exist… The words given in a dream initially meant nothing, until we typed them into a search engine. It was the healing centre of the classical world, in Greece, and did exist around the era of Cateus' story. It was a place where the sick went to be cured. To find the right cure for their ailments, they would sleep in the great hall, and, in their dreams, the gods would advise them on what to do to regain their health. Hygieia was the Greek goddess of health, cleanliness and the moon. She was the daughter of the Greek god of medicine, Asclepius. Hygieia's name is where our modern word 'hygiene' originated. She was associated more with the prevention of sickness and continuation of good health, which linked in nicely with what Cateus had told Dad concerning the naming of his daughter.

It is a fact that Mount Vesuvius did erupt in 79 AD, as recounted by Cateus in his story. On researching this evidence, the eruption tied in with the timeline of the character's ages, making it much more significant and, indeed, plausible!

It is also a fact that Gelligaer has a very prominent and well-recorded ancient history, which dates its occupancy back to the Bronze Age. It has obvious connections to the Romans, due to their 'historical footprint'.

In the photographs, you can see and validate the existence of the stones, with 'Maen Catwg' being the oldest indication of occupation in Gelligaer. What really intrigued us was the mystery stone of 'Waun-Y-Groes'. After reading some local literature about the Romans, there it was staring us in the face. 'Waun-Y-Groes' was another standing stone evident in Gelligaer, and originally stood between the churchyard and Dyffryn Park Estate with an 'Ogham' (Irish writing) inscription, but there has been no record of it since the mid eighteenth century.

What struck us was that this stone, possibly the one carried by the twin, existed, bizarrely, where the twin brother was rolled down the hill in the story.

It has been suggested that 'Maen Catwg' could be a capstone; if this is true, where is the evidence of what would have been an excavated burial, and why is it decorated? It has also been assumed that it's some sort of 'rock art'. This doesn't seem to add up either; rock art would have been captured at one significant time. The cup marks on 'Maen Catwg' are of different sizes and have weathered over time quite differently. Because of this, it seems obvious they would have been made at different times, making the theory of its role as a 'sacrificial stone' more apt. There are even details described in the story of when each mark was made and what each individual cup mark represented.

Each event seemed to happen for a reason. It was fate, and until certain events had passed Dad was unable to move onto the next chapter of the story. This suggests, to those who believe, that our lives are already mapped out for us. Initially, Dad found the coin in 1993; it had no significance until 2007. It wasn't until another Malcolm Rees had died and been buried on that significant spot that Dad started hearing the singing and experiencing the story. The other Malcolm Rees had died suddenly; there was no illness or reason for his sudden passing — we knew this because he was related to a friend of Dad's in the village. A man of the same name was buried on the very spot where Dad found the coin… Was this yet another coincidence?

Dad had often wondered about his name. His mother couldn't explain why they had chosen that name. Dad believed it was written in fate.

Strangely, my dad wanted to name me Hadrianne when I was born, but Mum disagreed and they chose to name me Nicola. If I had been named as my father wished, it would have been shortened to Hady! However, it is still funny how similar my name now sounds to Calla; Hadean was re-named Calla in the story.

Although there were many deaths that occurred in the events told, one significant factor was that *Medica* and her unborn child lived on to continue the Celtic bloodline.

No matter what one can assume from these events, I believe in my heart of hearts that my ancestry and that of my family involves these characters. I have lived with them over the past three years and have been touched deeply by their lives, and the stories told through my dad. I am proud of Bran's actions, his dedication to his homeland and the love he showed to his people. Bran was truly a powerful Druid in his ability to perform such magic and illusions, and to go beyond into the underworld and return unscathed.

It reminds me so much of my dad and his journey beyond the other side and his safe return. Is there really something special in our bloodline?

I certainly believe so.

NICOLA JONES

Nicola Jones is married with two daughters and resides in Deri, South Wales. Her passions include genealogy, the essence of nature and all things spiritual. This story was inspired by her father, Malcolm Jones, who has shared his story and journey.

Nicola has followed her father's footsteps, so to speak, and has become a spiritual healer. Coincidentally, one of Nicola's spiritual guides connects her and her father; Hygieia is now part of her journey.

You can keep up to date with Nicola on her Facebook fan page: Nicola Jones Author https://www.facebook.com/walkingintheirfootsteps/?-fref=ts

Publisher Information

Rowanvale Books provides publishing services to independent authors, writers and poets all over the globe. We deliver a personal, honest and efficient service that allows authors to see their work published, while remaining in control of the process and retaining their creativity. By making publishing services available to authors in a cost-effective and ethical way, we at Rowanvale Books hope to ensure that the local, national and international community benefits from a steady stream of good quality literature.

For more information about us, our authors or our publications, please get in touch.

www.rowanvalebooks.com
info@rowanvalebooks.com

Lightning Source UK Ltd.
Milton Keynes UK
UKHW021608230720
367020UK00006B/87